TRUSTED.TEAM

A Story of Known, Liked, and Trusted

I0402678

BY MARK PERONE

Trusted.Team A Story of Known, Liked, and Trusted © 2019 by Mark Perone

ISBN: 9781796280043

Imprint: Independently published

Printed in the United States of America

This is a work of fiction. Names, characters, businesses, places, events, locales, and incidents are either the products of the author's imagination or used in a fictitious manner. Any resemblance to actual persons, living or dead, or actual events is purely coincidental.

Dedication

It's important that we acknowledge time, present and past. Looking back, I see more people to appreciate than I can imagine, so I would like to give a nod to everyone who reads this book solely based on our association. Many will know what inspired certain depicted events and the basis for certain characters. Here's to being at the bottom, seeing the top, and everything in between.

This novel came to be, based on my desire to have something my daughter could know me by in her adulthood. At the time of this writing, she is four years old and will never know me as anyone aside from her father. My hope is that she reads this book and recognizes the hints within, having the ability to conceptualize the actual details of my life. It's an interesting thing being a parent. We are only who our children are able to perceive and what we allow them to see. I think it would be awesome to meet Cora as a stranger of the same age. This book may be that time traveling device.

There are a few more people I would like to call out in a shared paragraph, but Shelley Perone gets this one all to herself. I want to directly thank you for being you. All things considered, that is super generalized and very specific at the same time. Simply put, we live a full life together, and that makes me happy. I love you.

To the rest of that small group who has been around through the evolution of Mark E. Perone, I am doing what I said I would do to the best of my ability. Sometimes it's harder than it should be to stay friends. I love that you have given me the latitude to venture off on unblazed trails, some obviously the wrong way, and allowed me to stay in your lives. If you don't see yourself in the pages of this book, you might look harder or wait to read the next iteration. I'll get to you sooner than later. ;)

Last, I want to thank Joshua Lisec, Larry Turner, and Lee Autore for their support of this novel.

The skills I lack, you gentlemen more than cover. You fellas are just as much a part of this novel as I am. Without your intelligence, specific superpowers, and conceptual understanding, this project would not have made it off the runway. I truly believe we pulled together something special. Thanks for jumping in and taking on the challenge.

Contents

Preface

The very first words of mine I want you to read are those of appreciation. This is not meant to be a trite thank-you for taking the time and spending your hard-earned money. This is selfish appreciation. I am not a writer, novelist, or author by design, so thank you for allowing my ideas to hatch. It's short of a small miracle you're even holding my words in your mind right now. What an awesome thing.

That said, have you ever read a college textbook? They're boring. The author tries to teach ideas using stiff vocabulary and academic terminology. Textbooks are all concepts, theories, hypotheticals. . . except for the case studies. Here and there throughout the average textbook, authors explain their ideas through everyday situations. Now those are interesting. When the lessons include examples or illustrations, the textbook starts to resonate. Until the next page, at least. Then it's back to the boring academic language!

There is a category of books called "business fables." Think of these as case studies in narrative form. We meet different characters, hear their unique voices, and watch them interact. We see a part of us in each personality. By the end of the story, we've captured the author's idea, which was not just illustrated, but demonstrated through a multitude of perspectives. It's no wonder the top bestselling business books of all time have been, you guessed it, business fables.

While I was writing this book, countless colleagues, peers, and friends asked me, "What's your book about?" I always answered, "It's complicated," so as not to give away the ending. I will not do that here in the preface either. All I will reveal now is the message I want you to take away from this business fable:

The human condition is complicated. Our professions are one aspect of our lives, but the way we work has evolved in ways we don't even think about. Technology changed everything—for some of us. Others cling to the old ways of doing business, generating business, and sharing business.

What happens when the old ways clash with new ideas, new processes, new technology? Who gets the big wins? Who takes hard losses? To answer these questions, what type of business book do we need?

A business fable. I can't believe you're about to read my business fable. Especially because it's greater than the sum of its pages once you go from reading the story to living it in your own unique circumstances. The elements of secrecy and complex characters are just the hidden world of you and your friends' lives. Keep that thought in the back of your mind as the story unfolds.

Ultimately, this whole thing started because I have a serious problem with execution. I finally got irritated enough with common business interactions to write down what a successful one should look like. In the process, I learned how to achieve it. Reinforced with a drive to right some wrongs and connect people through human experience, I decided to guide curious people to a fantastic result. Yes, it's a business fable, but it's a story first. By the end, all this should crystallize.

Some of the events may be too perfect, but remember, everyone has their flow moments where the world aligns just right and dreams deliver themselves. I'm interested to see what you draw from the story. Nearly everyone who's read it before publication has had a unique perspective on how the story made them feel.

Just so we're clear, some version of what you're about to experience is true for all of us. If it hasn't happened to you yet, it could if you wanted it to. We are the ground that grew us, but our roots should never be limitations.

Good fortune!

Chapter 1

"Real estate? *Really?* Seriously?" Tucker grabbed the business card from Jamie's loose grip. "And when did you decide this was a good idea?"

"When I passed the prep course and aced the real estate exam in my business class." Jamie forced a smile. He looked past Tucker to the group of old friends seated around the table. "I'm a licensed real estate agent now. Licensed in New York. I passed the exam and everything."

"A *real* real estate agent. Well goooood work. Here's to you being all grown up!" Tucker took a long swallow of his vodka cranberry before sucking the last of the drink from the ice cubes. Last Christmas, he'd made it to ten or twelve drinks, depending on who was telling the story. That was right before Jamie fell into the role of human crutches, carrying his lanky frame home from the annual hometown meetup.

"Real estate, huh?" someone to Tucker's right said.

"Yeah, he sells houses 'n' shit. Isn't that right, Jamie?" Tucker put his hand on Jamie's right arm, giving him a rough, brotherly shake.

"Right." Jamie's shoulders tensed and lifted. "Some things have changed since last year. Hard to believe it's been that long since we've all seen one another." He glanced at each face around the table, pandering to the group. "So if anybody else wants a business card, I have mo—"

"*Dude!*" Tucker reached for Jamie's messenger bag. "You carry your business cards in a man purse? How. . . cosmopolitan!" Tucker laughed as he straightened an invisible bow tie.

"It's a satchel, thank you very little." Jamie rolled his eyes and pulled away from Tucker with a smile. Then he confidently passed a stack of fresh business cards around the table. "Like, you know. . . Indiana Jones."

Tucker held his now-empty glass up to the party. "To Indiana Jamie! My old roommate and my brand-new sales buddy. From being at the bottom, seeing the top, and everything in between!"

Jamie stole someone's untouched water, clinked it against half a dozen beers, and tapped it down on the table.

"*To the gods!*" Each member of the group stood, raising glasses into the air in a customary toast.

"So, Jamie. . . sold many houses yet?" said LaVell, an old friend of the former roommates. He and Jamie stood out as the only people in anything more formal than jeans.

"Um, well,"—Jamie swallowed—"I've got a few promising leads." He paused. All eyes were on him. "I'm doing okay. I mean, I just graduated and all."

"Don't call it 'graduating.'" Tucker emphasized the word by letting his glass hit the table. "C'mon, bro. You dropped out of college. Couldn't make it at a real school, so you settled for some certificate you got for a fall semester of business class." Tucker reached over and adjusted Jamie's collar. Jamie shot an annoyed glare at Tucker and pushed his hands away from his shirt. Tucker deflected with a spit-flinging *Psh!*

"Look, Jame," Tucker started again, speaking quietly only to Jamie, "it's okay to bomb in college. You just shot too high for yourself. Sales is the perfect place for guys like us to make our fortune." He turned back to the half-interested group. "Guess what? I've sold twenty-two Caddies at the dealership this month. Twenty. Two," he bragged with the oozing confidence of a sleazy car salesman.

"That's almost. . ." Jamie did the car sales commission math on his phone.

"That's a *lot*, baby!" Tucker slammed his glass on the table once more, loud enough to earn murmurs from the surrounding tables. "All I gotta do is average eighteen cars a month, and I'm the ten-million-dollar-a-year Cadillac salesman. And that's not gonna be a problem!"

"Well, that's easy for you, Tucker. You were born for that type of sales," Jamie said, waving at the server and gesturing to a beer on the table. "Real estate is more my game. Besides, every sale I make is probably ten times one of yours."

"Ooooooh." Tucker waved his hands in faux amazement. "It's your story, bro. So you tell it. You're dreaming; I'm living in reality. I do this every day," Tucker said. "All I'm saying is, I've got fifty people who are this close to buying from my dealership."

"Fifty people? Fifty prospects, you mean?" Jamie raised his eyebrows.

"Yeah, well, kind of. There's this business networking group I go to. Every Friday. With fifty members. LaVell's in it. He'll tell you." He waved his glass, rattling the ice cubes at the server for a refill. "It's a village ripe for pillaging, so to speak. Every person there is money in the bank."

"Pillaging? I wouldn't say all that!" LaVell laughed and shook his head. "More like a group of professionals who refer business to one another. It'd be great for you, too, just getting started. There's a good, solid group of people there to help you." LaVell sounded serious.

"It's working for us, right, LaVell?" Tucker said. "I found you that silver Mercedes you're picking up, right? Got you the financing and everything. All you have to do is show up, sign on the line that's dotted, and push the button to start on the road to freedom!"

"Well, yeah. That's the plan." LaVell looked back at Jamie, laughing. "At any rate, I think you would be a good addition to the group."

"Are you—" Jamie glanced at Tucker, then back to LaVell. "Are you guys inviting me? To a networking group?" He paused. "And what exactly is a networking group again?"

"No!" Tucker flung Jamie's business card at LaVell. It landed in the honey mustard. "I'm the one inviting you. Me. I brought it up. Plus, I'm the guy who invited you in the first place, LaVell. You got your membership because of me, remember?"

"Whoa, buddy." LaVell flashed another bright smile and put his hands up. "I remember." He tossed Jamie's yellowed card back at Tucker, missing him for Tucker's pile of boneless wings.

"Come on guys, I only ordered fifty cards. . ." Jamie trailed off.

"Dude, just come to the group tomorrow, and you'll make enough sales to order a hundred more. Maybe a thousand!" Tucker cackled. "A networking group is where a ton of business owners and sales guys show up to pitch their products to one another for an hour and a half." LaVell's eyes rolled. "We gotta try to make sure every industry in town is represented, and we still need a real estate guy. And it's only one person per profession allowed, so there's no competition within the group. So yeah, this is your lucky night! Tell you what,"—Tucker leaned in to Jamie and raised an eyebrow—"I'll personally introduce you to the group president."

"The president? I don't know, I've only been doing this for a few months."

"I thought you hadn't sold a house yet."

"Okay, fine." Jamie shrugged. "I haven't been doing this at all. I haven't really even started yet. I feel like I need to get a few sales closed before I—" He reached across Tucker's arm for his condiment-soaked card. "Just give me that back."

"Listen, seriously,"—Tucker swatted Jamie's hand—"we'll get you in the group, and maybe you'll be able to pass a rundown fixer-upper off onto somebody who doesn't know any better."

"Tucker,"—Jamie stiffened—"I think the real estate thing is a solid next step for me. You say you'll sell eighteen cars a month and hit like, what, ten million in sales?"

"Yeah, that's right." Tucker narrowed his eyes. "Care to make it interesting? I'll bet you can't cover ten mil in house sales this year."

Jamie took a hard swallow from his beer.

"Uh-oh!" LaVell clapped. "Did he just drop the mic on you, Jamie?"

Tucker grinned. "Not half as much as I dropped the mic this month. Check this out." Tucker shoved his hand into his back pocket and thumped a wad of bills onto the table.

Jamie gaped. "Holy sh—"

"This is just one week, man. One. Week. Better hope people start fleeing the city so home prices go up around here. That's all I'm saying."

"Maybe that vodka pickled your brain, Tucker." Jamie reached out his hand. "You're on. First to ten million this year wins. Even with that head start." He side-eyed Tucker's cash.

"Deal." Tucker slapped his palm into Jamie's, and they shook on it.

"Wins what? What are y'all betting?" LaVell asked.

Jamie and Tucker exchanged blank looks.

"You wanna bet cash?" Tucker said, swirling his glass and lightly rattling the ice cubes. "Probably not a good idea though, since you're a newb."

"Don't you still owe him from your last bet, Tucker?" someone shouted from across the table, and a couple of guys broke out laughing.

"Old news. Five hundo good for you?" Tucker said quickly.

"Let's make it an even 'G.' A one and three zeros."

Tucker laughed. "Easiest grand I'll ever make. Hey, I've got an idea. The least I can do is help you catch up, Jamie. Maybe we do an open house and set up the old beer bong. Case races. End the night with the box game!" Tucker's eyebrows wagged up and down.

"Right. Fantastic idea," Jamie said.

"Yeah, and legendary!" Tucker grabbed Jamie around the neck. "Like back at the apartment? We'd crush a twelve-pack before parties and toss full beers off the balcony to the neighbors . . . good times."

"Yeah, and I'd mop up the drunk people. I remember." Jamie nodded. "I have no interest in repeating that." He looked at LaVell. "So, LaVell, when and where's this networking group? Tomorrow morning? What time?"

"I'll text you. Don't worry about it." Tucker dismissed Jamie and stood up. "All right, guys! Let's cash out. One check. Let's call it belated Friendsgiving, Merry Xmas, whatever. It's time to move on!" Tucker waved at everyone like a quarterback pumping up the crowd. "First round of drinks at the Cubby Hole is on me. Who's in?"

"Sorry," Jamie cut in, "I appreciate the beer, but I want to be ready to meet people in the morning. And I have a new phone number, so keep my card."

Tucker cupped his hands around his mouth. "*Boo!* What kind of bullshit is that?"

"I'm serious. You said this networking group thing could be a big deal for me. February is right around the corner, so . . ."

"Yeah, dude, because I'll be there." Tucker winked, then addressed everyone, collecting coats and purses from the backs of chairs. "And we ride!"

"Good to see you again, Jamie." LaVell offered a friendly handshake before jogging off toward Tucker. "Hope to see you in the morning."

"You too. And yeah, I'll be there." Jamie sat down to finish his beer. Tucker weaved through the back of the restaurant, flung open the patio door wide, and hopped the fence. The group of friends following him used the gate to exit.

After a few handshakes, short hugs, and waves, everyone said goodbye.

"You all finished here?" a busser yelled from behind Jamie's shoulder.

"I'm going to finish this." Jamie held up his beer.

The busser ignored him, scraping plates, cups, and silverware from the table into his plastic tub.

"Hey, wait a second." Jamie stood up. "Are those. . . my business cards?"

Scattered among the half-eaten entrees and balled-up napkins were the business cards he'd passed around.

"Hold up, hang on!" Jamie leaped out of his chair and reached for the cards directly in front of the busser. "These aren't trash."

The busser waited for Jamie to salvage the dozen cards nobody wanted.

Then Jamie spotted it.

Still sporting mustard.

The card he'd given Tucker.

He'd left his too.

"Great. Just great." Jamie slumped back into his chair with a heavy sigh. He shot back up and peered through the window. Maybe—

No. They were long gone. Probably ordering the first round of shots.

Jamie pulled out his phone and pressed the speech-to-text search button.

"Networking groups near me, Friday mornings, what time?"

Chapter 2

"'Helping you find your dream home. . . ' 'Helping you find your dream home. . . ' 'Helping. . . '" Jamie recited his tagline as he drove. "Cheesy. 'Helping you find a pretty good place to live.' Even worse." He checked his face in the rearview mirror. "Come on, Jamie. You aren't really nervous. Get your professional on!"

He reached down to straighten his tie, which wasn't there. "Great. Forget 'Helping.' 'Cheap suit, cheap homes.' Much better, Jamie." He pulled into the parking lot five minutes early and took a space in the back of the lot, a whole row away from the other networkers' cars.

"'Helping you find your dream home.'" Jamie reverted to the original. He grabbed last night's forgotten business cards from the cup holder, drew in a deep breath, and stepped out of his sedan.

A wall of cigarette odor stopped him midstep.

Tucker.

"Oh, hey!" Jamie cleared his throat. "Didn't see you. How was last night?"

"Legendary. As always. You know me!" Tucker grinned slyly before letting out a solid exhale of smoke. "Speaking of legendary, here's my plan." His head bobbed toward the two-story office building as they started walking.

"See everybody's rides here? I've been staking 'em out." Tucker and Jamie passed a Lexus, a Charger, and then a Jeep. "I get here early, see who's driving what, then I chat people up on the latest models on my floor. Easy sales, baby."

"Cool."

"Uh, yeah! Totally cool. Isn't it a great plan? 'Cause I think it's a great plan."

Jamie kept his gaze on the asphalt, whispering his elevator pitch and tagline.

"You nerd," Tucker said, sharply flicking his cigarette onto the asphalt. "You'll do fine." He flung the door open and motioned for Jamie to enter first with a slight bow. "Happy pillaging."

Networkers in everything from business suits to T-shirts and jeans huddled around a check-in table next to a standing cardboard sign.

"THE NETWORK OF AMERICAN BUSINESS"

"Step one, show up at the right place. Check," Jamie muttered, stepping into line.

"Forget this. I got you." Tucker motioned for Jamie to follow, cutting past networkers waiting their turn.

"Jamie! Jamie Morris!" someone called from behind the check-in table.

"Oh, hi! How are you, Ray?" Jamie stopped. Tucker kept walking. "Funny seeing you here. I guess you're a member?"

"You might say that." Ray laughed and reached out a hand. "I'm president of this bunch, actually."

"President? Wow!" Jamie accepted the shake, then glanced back at the line he skipped. "So, what do we do here? Sign in and pay, or. . ."

"There's no cost to visit. Just step over here in line, and we'll get you—"

"Jamie, let's go!" Tucker doubled back to check in. "Oh, hey, Ray-Ray. You guys know each other?"

"Yes!" Ray smiled. "From church."

Tucker's face twisted like he'd just eaten a lemon.

"You go to church now? Really? Since when?"

"Since a while ago." It was Jamie's turn to check in. "So, Ray, where do I sign in?"

Tucker left the two for breakfast in the conference room.

"Welcome to the Network of American Business," Ray said. "I'll give a quick overview of our group when we start. What we're all about. Then everyone does their own thirty-second elevator pitch so we get to know one another's businesses better. You'll go last since you're a visitor."

"Perfect, thank you." Jamie shook Ray's hand again.

Jamie spotted Tucker sitting next to LaVell at one of a dozen folding circular tables on the far side of the room. Tucker passed around dealership brochures featuring the newest Lexus, Charger, Jeep, and other models.

"Dude, you missed it!" Tucker hailed Jamie. "Sale number twenty-three!" His arms shot up into the touchdown signal.

"Hold on there, buddy." LaVell looked up from a brochure. "All we did was get a one to one on the schedule."

"You want a new ride, don't you?"

"Well, yeah. Can't keep hitching rides in my wife's truck all the time. A photographer without a car is a photographer without a business."

"Boom." Tucker pumped his fist into his palm. "Good as sold."

Before Jamie could chime in or grab a coffee, Ray called the meeting to order.

"Good morning, everyone! And welcome. For those of you who are new to the Network of American Business, we're a business referral group, not a social group. We believe in long-term relationship building with an emphasis on getting ahead by giving referrals. As most of you know, we track the referrals every member gives and the corresponding business. See the triplicate slips on your tables?" He grabbed a yellow, blue, and white slip from a plastic carton at the nearest table. "We all fill these out, tallying the details every week, including our invited visitors." He smiled at Jamie. "Referrals received, closed business, and referrals given. The leadership committee adds up everyone's numbers, and we keep a running annual total."

"Huh. Carbon copy paper," Jamie whispered to Tucker. "Old school. I kinda like it."

"Not half as much as you'll like Catherine." Tucker eyes locked on someone a few tables over.

"Who's Catherine?"

Tucker pointed to the table directly across the room. Five total networkers, one woman.

Catherine. Probably old enough to have gray hair, but her blonde highlights concealed it well. Her tailored black-and-white pantsuit made her look like a trial lawyer next to the other networkers at her table, all tradesmen whose monogrammed hoodies and polos featured business logos with a generic last name followed by "LLC."

"Catherine," Jamie breathed. She was striking.

"She always goes first," Tucker whispered. "An old-school hottie, isn't she? Like, teacher hot. Or nurse hot."

"Come on, I'm trying to listen!" Jamie whispered.

"Bro, I'd totally listen to her, if you know what I mean!"

"Shhh!"

The thirty-second commercials commenced. Catherine stood. Tucker elbowed Jamie's arm.

"Catherine Hawthorn, president of Rethink Revenue," she began, making quick eye contact with the networkers at the surrounding tables. "Everyone who knows me knows I'm not very self-promotional. I'd rather educate than advertise. And that's what we do at Rethink Revenue. Almost everyone here is already one of our clients on some level, so most of you have gotten that education." She side-eyed Jamie.

"We sell software solutions to help build long-term relationships with customers, but we're really all about helping turn initial sales into second, then third opportunities. We all know the second sale is always easier than the first, right?" She made eye contact with Jamie and paused slightly. "Our business software solutions, starting with customer relationship management, also help identify prospects who are most likely to buy. We believe the right setup is far more effective than the most diligent follow-up. Have you heard the saying, 'It's not what you know; it's who you know'? We take that a step further to emphasize 'how' someone is known. Does that person need what you're selling right now, and do they know that?" Her gaze fell on Jamie again. He took refuge in an incoming text message that he didn't actually receive.

"Is she looking at me or you?" Tucker whispered.

"Shhh!"

"Our clients execute exponential growth by understanding their perfect customers' information and activities from previous client journeys." Catherine's voice lowered. "Imagine being able to hold your business and its stakeholders accountable to a focused process. And they appreciate you for it. We rethink revenue to expedite true value for client journeys, creating a method to quality client interaction. Focus on known and liked to become trusted. I am Catherine Hawthorn. Our standard at Rethink Revenue: increasing revenue while lowering the cost of doing business."

"Wow." Jamie leaned toward Tucker as Catherine sat down. "I need what she's selling."

"While you're busy with that, I'll have *her*."

Jamie smacked Tucker's forearm. "I mean the software she's talking about. The customer referral management? What was it?"

"It's CRM. Stands for 'client revenue manager' or something, I think."

Everyone looked at Tucker. He glanced at the member sheet on the table.

"Guess I'm up!"

Tucker bolted upright, a brochure in each hand. "Let me ask you all a question. What if I told you I could get you in this,"—he gracefully flipped open a Cadillac brochure, revealing a fleet of luxury vehicles—"or this,"—he showed off a Mercedes-Benz brochure in the other hand—"in one of six of the hottest colors? And what if I told you I could finance any credit tier, guaranteed? Good credit, bad credit, I don't care. I just want your money!" Waves of chuckling washed over the group. "Let me get you a sweet monthly payment on one of these. Based on what's out in the parking lot, a lot of you guys could use an upgrade." More laughter. "Listen, I'm gonna treat you to a once-in-a-lifetime opportunity. Come on down to my dealership, and I'll put you behind the wheel of something that makes you feel like a million bucks."

Beaming with the charming sarcasm of a spotlight showman, Tucker pulled his chair out to sit back down. "See me after the meeting," he whispered to Jamie.

"Good job." Jamie nodded.

Following the member sheet order, everyone else stood and offered their thirty-second spiels. Jamie spent the next twenty minutes scribbling updated iterations of his elevator pitch to fill his allotted time, adding showy industry terms he'd picked up from his real estate course textbook, like, "truth-in-lending disclosure" and "sales comparison approach."

"Thanks, everyone. Okay!" Ray stood up after the last member's commercial. "I know we have a visitor this morning. Jamie? Tell us a little about yourself."

Jamie pushed back his chair, keeping his eyes on the member sheet turned script.

"Uh, hi." He silently read the first sentence again. And again. "Hi, everyone. I'm Jamie. I'm a real estate agent. And I help you find your dream home."

Jamie looked up. Across the room. His eyes met Catherine's.

"Everyone who knows me knows I'm not super salesy." Jamie went off script. "I'd rather help people than pitch them."

Catherine smiled.

Jamie's shoulders rose. "Let me paint you a picture. Imagine coming home to a place that actually feels like home. Not a house. Or an apartment. Or a condo, or whatever. A home. And it's yours, not some landlord's. Your home feels like bare feet on freshly vacuumed carpet. It sounds like family. It smells of warm memories. Your home tastes like your favorite fresh-baked brownie. It's as stress-free as a vacation rental on the beach, but you never have to leave. The place feels like you." He cleared his throat. "That's what

I do. I help you find that feeling, your sense of home. Thank you."

"Dude!" Tucker said. "Lay off the tear-jerking."

Ray dismissed everyone to open networking. LaVell reached an open palm across the table. "Actually, Jamie, can I get your card again? We should talk. My wife and I are in the market."

"For a car," Tucker interjected.

"Well, I am. But you know Cornell. She's been on my case for us to get out of that dive on the east side for over a year now."

"Okay, sure! Here you go." Jamie handed LaVell a beer-stained card.

"Aww, look at that." Tucker dabbed a napkin under his eye. "Jamie's first referral."

"Please! I've had referrals before."

"*Psh!* Likely story."

"Listen," LaVell interrupted, "I'm serious about this home thing. I like what you said about the dream home and childhood memories and whatnot. And Cornell just got a promotion, so—"

"So two brand-new S-Class Mercedeses for you guys," Tucker said. "Right?"

"Well, I'm sure I can help," Jamie said. "Have you guys been to any open houses or have an eye on any particular listings? Any ideas on neighborhood, size, or layout?"

"I know we want to move farther from downtown. I'm not really sure on the specs, but I do know our price range. Well, I *knew* our price range before her promotion. I'm hoping for an acre or so with a basement. We definitely want more than two bedrooms."

Jamie pulled out his phone, clicked an app, and handed it to LaVell. "There's a new listing you guys might like. Just on the market this week. Three bedroom, two-and-a-half bath, gorgeous interior, plenty of trees. . ."

LaVell's eyes widened. "That's right up our alley. Where is it?"

"Like, fifteen minutes from here. Quiet neighborhood. Suburbia. Do you have some time right now? I've got the lockbox code. Maybe Cornell could meet us for lunch or something, and we could do a quick walk through."

"Wait! You're supposed to come with me to the dealership. We scheduled our meeting, remember?" Tucker snapped. "You can't back out."

"We can always reschedule that, right?" LaVell scrolled through the photos on Jamie's phone. "Let me see if she can meet us. She works close by."

"But I've already got your paperwork ready," Tucker said. "And I'm really cutting into my own commission for you. A *lot*."

LaVell texted his wife without looking up.

Tucker cleared his throat. "You know, I'm not a pushy kinda guy, but the boss says I can't offer a deal like this for more than a couple of days."

"Actually, she can meet us now!" LaVell pocketed his phone. "Do you still have her number? Can you send her the link? I want her to look at the listing. She can leave work and meet us there. I'd give her ten minutes. I'll ride with you?"

"Uh, sure," Jamie said. "But do you, you know. . ."

Tucker threw up his arms. Not a touchdown this time.

"Do you and Tucker want to reschedule first, or. . ."

Tucker stormed off.

"I guess not."

While LaVell shook a few colleagues' hands, Jamie grabbed a coffee to go.

"Would've liked to give the CRM lady my card," Jamie said to LaVell on the way out, no Catherine in sight.

"See you next week, Jamie?" Ray called from the check-in table.

"I'll be here!" Jamie shouted back.

About ten minutes later, Jamie and LaVell pulled into the driveway of a contemporary-style house with white siding, green shutters, and a three-car garage. A pair of weeping willows guarded each side of the front entry.

Cornell's station wagon was already in the driveway.

"How did you find this? I love it already!" she called out, scouting the property's front lawn. "I hadn't seen this one listed. Jamie, this is an awesome find!"

Cornell greeted Jamie with a tight squeeze of a hug. "I went around back. The yard is great. It's landscaped and shouldn't take much time to mow."

Jamie punched in the lockbox code and ushered the couple inside. "Welcome to the rest of your life. As you can see, this home greets you with a spacious front foyer, warm three-quarters-inch acacia hardwood flooring throughout, family-style kitchen with plenty of room for birthday and holiday parties, and an open-concept dining room transition into the living room."

Cornell disappeared into the empty living room. "*Two* fireplaces. One in the kitchen! Who has that? This one looks just like my grandmother's house! Oh, I *love* this brick." Cornell's bangles and bracelets reverberated around the first floor.

"Cool, why don't you show yourselves around?" Jamie said.

"She's in love," LaVell said. "Guess I better be careful!"

"Just wait 'til she sees the granite countertops and natural stone backsplash in the kitchen. Freakin' gorgeous." Jamie led LaVell to the garage. "Now check this out." Jamie flicked on the light switch. "Three-car garage with cabinets for all your tools, chipped-finish concrete coating, and plenty of space for that Mercedes you and Tucker picked out."

"Well, that's the problem," LaVell said. "I didn't want to tell Tucker yet, but. . . I don't see Cornell going for a new house and a new car at the same time. I mean, we've made do with just hers for a couple of years now. I want to expand the business, but most weddings and graduations and whatnot are on weekends when the car's mine."

"But you told Tucker—"

"I know, I know. Tucker's wanting me to go through on the Mercedes. I haven't told Cornell about it yet. Was going to once I saw what kind of monthly payments we were looking at."

Jamie's phone buzzed.

It buzzed again.

A phone call.

Tucker.

"You get that. I'ma talk to Cornell about all this."

Jamie waited in the garage but didn't answer. No voice mail. Another buzz. A text.

"Done yet? LaVell on his way here?"

Jamie mouthed his response as he typed. "No. . . still . . . here . . ."

Something like a cough or a laugh came from the living room. Jamie shoved his phone into his pocket without sending the message and followed after LaVell.

"Hell no, that ain't happening!" Jamie caught the middle of Cornell's rant. "The house is a *need*. The car is a *want*. We've looked at a number of houses, and this is the one."

"Okay, okay, I got you." LaVell put his arm around her. "A house it is. What about a used car maybe?"

"Maybe. A *big* maybe. Just because we have a three-car garage doesn't mean—" She turned. "Hey, Jamie. Are we the first to see this place?"

"That's right. First and only." Jamie smiled.

"Then let's be the last. We wanna make an offer. Right now."

"Really? Great! Okay, let me get some paperwork from the car. Well, I think it's in my car. Hang on." He jogged to the front door.

"Take your time!" Cornell laughed. "But hurry up. I don't want somebody else coming by and snatching my dream home, you know what I'm saying?"

"Yeah, I know what you're saying. Just a minute."

Alone on the porch, Jamie deleted his draft to Tucker and typed a new reply.

"IDK. They want to make offer. Say they can't afford both."

Before he pressed "Send," LaVell's phone went off. It went silent after one ring. He must not have answered.

"Damnit," Jamie muttered.

Then his own phone buzzed. Tucker. Jamie took a deep breath and swiped to answer.

"Hey, Tucker, I got your text. I'm not really sure if they're coming to the dealership. They want to put in an offer on the house. Cornell loves it. But they can't afford both, it sounds like." Jamie dropped every update at once. "I'll let you know how everything turns out. Okay?"

"Both? What do you mean both? Huh? Huh?"

Jamie migrated farther from the porch. "Both a new car and a new house. Cornell really likes this place, but it's kinda pricey. I haven't seen their offer yet, but—"

"Whatever, dude. Congrats. You just stole my sale. I bring you to the networking group, and you steal my freakin' sale on your first damn day!"

"Hang on, nothing's been signed yet."

LaVell peeked outside. "Got that paperwork?"

"Yeah, just a minute!" Jamie held one finger up. "Nothing's official yet." He lowered his voice. "And I put in a good word for that Mercedes."

"Shut up. Was that LaVell? Put him on. I need to talk to him."

"We can all talk later." Jamie fumbled his car keys with one hand. "I've gotta go be all customer servicey now."

"Fine. I've got options for LaVell to look at anyway. I'll put him in something before Sunday. Just you watch."

Tucker hung up.

Jamie crossed his arms over the top of his car and dropped his head.

"Damnit."

Chapter 3

The meeting was about to start. Jamie hurried into the conference room from check-in with the other stragglers.

He cleared his throat as he approached Tucker from behind.

"Hey! So, how was your week?"

Tucker didn't look up from his phone.

"Did you get a chance to reschedule your one-on-one with LaVell? He seemed really interested last week."

Now Tucker looked up. *"No."* He shoved both hands into his pockets. "I've still got a Mercedes to sell. Know anyone?"

Jamie took the open seat next to Tucker. "Look, I feel really bad about what happened. I mean, they made the offer, and it looks like it's gonna be my first real sale. And you're already doing so well and—"

"Because I don't expect people I trust to steal from me," Tucker huffed. "You owe me. You owe me *big*."

"Okay, okay. I'll be sure to put in a good word for you today in my commercial."

"Whatever, dude."

"All right, everyone!" Ray called from the main table. "Welcome to Networkers of American Business. I'm glad to see some familiar faces back this week." He nodded at Jamie. "For those of you who are new here, we're a business referral group."

While Ray stuck to the script, LaVell scored breakfast: donuts and coffee. Jamie waved for him to join their table. LaVell's eyes darted between Jamie and Tucker. He grabbed an open seat at the table next to Jamie.

After Ray finished the opener, Catherine stood for her thirty-second turn.

"Hey," Tucker whispered to Jamie. "Tell LaVell to come to the dealership this weekend. I'll get him a deal on something used. Used but classy."

"Sure. Yeah. I'll talk to him."

Catherine finished. Tucker's turn.

"Hey, guys. No brochures this week. It's been a great month at the dealership. Not so much a good week. Sometimes you just can't trust people. They'll lead you on and throw you away. But I guess that's business."

Jamie peered over at LaVell, who stuffed the rest of his donut into his mouth.

"So I guess what I need from you guys today," Tucker continued, "is to get some one to ones with you on the schedule so I can tell you about all the new models we've gotten. I've got this sweet Escalade I can see about half of you driving. All right, that's it."

When the next NAB member stood, Tucker piped back up, "Remember, guys! I need some one to ones. See me after!"

Like last week, the networkers each gave their commercial before the visitors' turns. Jamie, again the sole visitor, stood.

"Hi again, everyone. Jamie, independent real estate agent." He paused. "I just want to tell you how grateful I am for this group. I'm not even a member yet, and my first referral from last week turned into a sale." He pointed down at Tucker. "My friend Tucker's been awesome. He invited me here, and I'm super glad he did. By the way, you really should meet with him after and check out the deals he can get you on a Mercedes. Tucker's great at what he does." Tucker didn't acknowledge the praise. "So I guess. . ." His eyes met Catherine's across the room. "I guess something Catherine said last week stuck with me. It's Catherine, right?" She nodded. "You said something last week like, 'It's not who you know; it's how you know them.' I definitely felt that working with my referred client this week. So thank you, everyone. Thanks, Tucker." Jamie smiled at Catherine. "And thank you, Catherine." She smiled back. "Hope you accept my membership. I'm turning in the application today. Thanks!"

"Look at you," Tucker whispered. "Puttin' the moves on her! The hell, man?"

"What?"

"Already stole from me once, dude. Back off."

"We're glad to see you back, Jamie!" Ray called from the front. "All right, everyone. No announcements this week. Be sure to write down your referrals and turn them in here or at check-in. Have a great weekend!"

Tucker bolted upright. "Grab LaVell. I've got a hot date tonight." He started toward Catherine's table. "Just got to hammer out the details."

"Hey, buddy!" LaVell said to Jamie before he could respond to Tucker. "That was a cool shout-out you gave."

"Yeah, thanks!" Jamie shook his hand. "It's a great group for sure." LaVell didn't say anything immediately, so he jumped back in. "Anyway, how are things coming with the bank? Sure wish everyone was preapproved like you and Cornell."

"Right? Like I said, I mean, this house thing has been on Cornell's mind for a while. And when you said what you did last week about the dream home, I just knew—"

"Catherine's busy. Hey, LaVell!" Tucker interrupted. "Man, you've gotta get your phone checked. I've been trying to get ahold of you to reschedule our meeting. I've got this great used Caddy you'd look like a boss rolling through town in."

"Uh. . . maybe. Maybe we can do that," LaVell said.

Jamie backed away from the awkwardness.

"Any coffee left?" he said to no one in particular on the short walk to the breakfast table.

Jamie concentrated on the coffee pouring into his tiny Styrofoam cup. The conversation he escaped continued on without him. He reached for the sugar and cream.

Knock. Knock. Knock.

"What's that noise?" Jamie turned around. No stray networkers responded. Everyone nearby looked occupied exchanging business cards.

"Anybody else hear that?" Jamie said, again to no one specific. "Sounded like somebody knocking. What's that?"

Jamie left his black coffee on the breakfast table. Somebody's business card lay on top of his messenger bag at his seat. A quadruple-thick black business card.

Jamie picked it up. "Weird." A debossed title appeared on the card, front and center in thick gold lettering. "Trusted.Team."

Jamie picked at the corner of the card, which was thick enough to have been three or even four cards stacked together. He flipped it over. On the otherwise blank side was a small indentation in the lower right corner. He turned the card back and forth to catch the light, and the text "/One" appeared in a small rubbery font.

Jamie held up the business card to the nearest networking threesome—an electrician, insurance agent, and work-from-home direct marketer. "This belong to anyone? Any of yours?"

All nos and head shakes.

"Hey, guys." Jamie turned back to Tucker and LaVell. "Either of you know whose this is? Somebody laid it on my bag. And did you hear that. . . knocking?"

"Let me see that." Tucker snatched the card from Jamie and examined it. "Could be one of those scams. 'Trusted dot team? Slash one?'" Tucker flipped the card over and back. "Nope. No idea."

"Nah, I don't recognize the name," LaVell said. "Maybe there was a meeting before ours. Another networking group?"

"I don't know. I'll look into it later." Jamie scanned the networkers filtering out. "Did Catherine leave yet? Still haven't shaken her hand."

Tucker shot him a glare.

"I think exchanging cards would be a good idea. Sounds like she might know a lot of people. People with homes to sell. Or buy."

"Yeah, right. But me first," said Tucker, hurrying off.

"All right then." LaVell chuckled.

Jamie and LaVell traded goodbyes and joined fellow networkers on the exodus from the conference room. Still no Catherine. Tucker headed outside with a cigarette.

"I'll ask around," Jamie said to Tucker. "See who I know that's in the market for your deal of the month."

Tucker flashed a thumbs-up. "Yeah, okay, dude. LaVell and I rescheduled. So I guess we're cool. As long as you keep your hands off Catherine. Been setting her up for a while now. Don't blow it for me."

Jamie rolled his eyes. "Please Tucker, I just wanted a contact. Nothing unprofessional ever even crossed my mind."

Tucker's eyes narrowed. "Yeah. Sure."

When Jamie returned to his home office—a desk, laptop, and folding chair in his studio apartment—he dove into the stack of closing paperwork for LaVell and Cornell. Due diligence kept him behind the desk through lunch. And then dinner.

After sundown, a text from Tucker shook him out of the zone.

"Found something. Call me."

Jamie accepted the break from work and hit the "Call" button. "What's up?"

"Did you know?" Tucker said with a mouthful of crunch, probably chips. "Dot com isn't the only website address you can have."

"What are you talking about?"

"That business card. The 'Trusted Team' thing. It's a website. You in front of your computer?"

"Uh, yeah." Jamie opened a new browser tab. "It's a website?"

"It's like trusted dot com, but it's trusted dot team."

Jamie typed the unusual address, "T-r-u-s-t-e-d-dot-t-e-a-m" and pressed "Enter" to be directed to _Trusted.Team_. "You're right. It's just a blank page with a gold key in the middle." Jamie clicked the key. "Wait a sec. Now the cursor is like. . . like a flashlight."

"Dude, you're right," Tucker said. "Looks like one of those old computer games we had as kids."

"What are these?" Jamie clicked around. "It looks like. . . books? Bookshelves? Freaky. You know those search games from back in the day, where you had to click to find the hidden objects?" Jamie randomly moved his cursor around different sections of the screen, revealing the books' blurry titles. A keyhole revealed itself on screen. "Wow! It is one of those mystery games. Do you see that keyhole?" Jamie clicked the keyhole. The static page came alive—the bookshelves parted in half, and a text box appeared on his screen. "Holy. . ."

"What? What do you see?" Tucker barked. "Dude, where's the keyhole?"

"It's like a card catalog drawer. I'm supposed to type something in it. I think," Jamie said. "There's a forward slash."

"A slash? Like on the back of the card, 'Slash One'?"

"Slash One?" Jamie said. "Oh! Where did I put that card?" Jamie put Tucker on speakerphone and rummaged through his satchel.

"What happens if you type 'One' and hit 'Enter'?"

"Oh, right." Jamie returned to the keyboard. He typed the word and pressed "Enter."

The screen went blank. Then another page appeared. A black background with gold text in fancy vintage letters.

"It's text. Like, old-timey text. Says, 'Personal invitation extended to you by Slash One.' And there's a picture of. . . Catherine?"

"What? Catherine? Who the hell is 'Slash One'?"

"Whoever gave me that card, I'm assuming," Jamie said. "Wherever it is." He kept reading. "'Thank you for responding to—'" He stopped.

"To what? To *what*?"

"It says. . ." Jamie swallowed. "It says, 'Thank you for responding to Catherine's invitation.'"

"Catherine? *My* Catherine?" Tucker's voice cracked semisarcastically. "Dude, it's going to be some *Eyes Wide Shut* orgy thing. You're taking me with you."

"Definitely not." Jamie skimmed the paragraphs under the heading. "It's an invitation to become a prospect in a 'strategic partnership' thing. It says, 'The Trusted Team is on a quest, and we hope you become our next valuable asset. Within the Trusted Team, we find appropriate ways to introduce partners to new sales opportunities as subject-matter experts, willing to add their value in ways others do not.' Wow."

"So it's some kind of exclusive business club?"

"Maybe." Jamie scanned the last paragraph. "'You've been invited to join the Trusted Team because Slash One believes you exemplify our Keys of Success.'"

"Keys of success? You just made your first freakin' sale, dude. I've sold like, thirty cars this month. I'm the damn closer here!"

"Hang on." Jamie frowned. "It says Catherine has a profile on here." He clicked the hyperlink. A thumbnail image of Catherine's headshot appeared. "'Trusted Team Member Metrics,'" Jamie read the accompanying details. "This can't be right. It says here Catherine's sold over fifteen million through this team thing—just this year!"

"Oh, that's total BS!" Tucker laughed. "Nobody in our group sells like that. What does she even sell?"

"She sells software, so maybe it's possible. Like I said, I want what she's selling."

"So why'd she invite you, huh? I could do fifteen million by now in Lexus sales if I worked at the Long Island dealership, easy."

"Tucker, do you think this is for real? I mean, why would they have all this information on here?" Jamie said. "This looks like some type of secret business group or something, which would be pretty cool. Or is it a joke? Or some kind of initiation into the NAB group?"

"If it is, I haven't heard about it. I feel like I would know, since I've closed like a billion dollars in business since I started with NAB. So you're seriously interested in this? I already called Catherine, bro. I have dibs. Remember, I invited you. Stick with NAB. Just ignore this. . . this scam, or joke, or club, or whatever it is."

Jamie ignored the protest. "It says the next step is to put in my contact info, social media profiles, and pay fifty bucks to apply."

"There it is! Scam. I told you! Catherine's as smart as she is sexy. That's how she keeps herself in those designer suits."

Jamie was silent. His fingers rattled across the keyboard.

"Um, hello?"

"Yeah," Jamie said. "Typing my email and links and stuff. I'm gonna do this. I'm gonna apply."

"No, you're not! C'mon man, it's late. Let's go get a beer and hit on the college chicks at Chappy's."

"I'm serious." Jamie entered his debit card info on the page. "And no, I'm not up for tonight. Maybe tomorrow. . ."

"Loser. She's scamming you. We both know it."

"Seriously? It's fifty dollars. I'm willing to risk it."

"Whatever. You'll see. You change your mind tonight, you know where I'll be." Tucker hung up.

Jamie clicked the "Submit" button.

Before the confirmation page loaded, his phoned buzzed. Then again. And again. And again.

It wasn't a phone call.

It was a text message, an email, and messages to every social media profile.

"That was fast," Jamie muttered.

"Jamie: we appreciate your effort thus far. Your Trusted. Team journey is unfolding./One has selected you as a prospect for the Trusted Team. Type Next Steps for more information."

Thumbing "Next Steps," Jamie obeyed and responded to the text.

His phone went crazy again, the same message coming in on every platform.

Catherine's name, an appointment date and time, and an address.

"Tomorrow at five a.m.? Seriously?" Jamie blurted out loud. He opened the coordinates on his GPS app. Downtown Manhattan. A two-hour commute.

"You have got to be kidding." He shook his head.

His phone buzzed again. A text from Tucker.

"NVM about Chappy's. Drinks and pool next door. Tons of hot chicks here!!!"

Seconds later, another.

"BTW I hit multiple six figs for the year today. Killing this bet. #winning."

Jamie didn't reply. To either text. He powered off his laptop, set his alarm for two a.m., and headed into the bathroom to get ready for bed.

"Catherine," he breathed, "what are you up to?"

Chapter 4

"You have arrived," the GPS proclaimed.

"About damn time," Jamie huffed, checking the time on the dash. Three minutes till five.

He parallel parked his sedan and dumped two handfuls of car nickels and dimes into the parking meter.

"I guess this is it," he said as a stream of pedestrians flowed by. Last night's instructions had kept the name of his destination a surprise. "'New York Brewmasters Guild Number One,'" he read the old-fashioned font aloud. The brewpub logo featured a bare-chested, handlebar-mustachioed boxer chugging a pint.

"So Catherine's a closeted hipster. Great," Jamie muttered, heading inside the reclaimed packing plant during a break in foot traffic.

He scanned the occupied tables for Catherine, but there was no sign of her. Just a few yuppies staring at tablets while eating breakfast and sipping coffee.

Jamie took a stool at the bar. The bartender looked like the boxer, except for the piercings and fully tattooed arm.

"Hey," Jamie said. "Any menus around here?"

The bartender gave him an up-down and reached underneath the copper bar top.

"You'll be needing this." He slid a palm-size block of wood across the bar. A bronze skeleton key dangled from an attached piece of yarn.

"A bathroom key? Food's that bad, huh?" Jamie chuckled.

The bartender didn't smile.

"Do we know each other?" Jamie slowly pushed the key away.

The bartender turned away without a word, facing the mounted wall mirror.

"Okay then. So. . . can I get a menu or—"

"Around the corner." The bartender's gaze shot up to meet Jamie's in the mirror above his head. "And take the key with you."

Jamie slid off the stool. "Wait a second. You don't happen to know Cath—"

"Around the corner," the bartender repeated. With an outreached arm, he pointed to Jamie's left, where a vintage neon sign blinked, directing patrons to the restrooms.

Jamie got up and scanned the restaurant one more time. No Catherine. The clock above the bar read 5:02.

He picked up the key and followed the bartender's instruction.

Sure enough, there were men's and women's restrooms.

"What the—"

Neither door had a lock. Or a handle.

"Around the corner. . ." Jamie whispered the bartender's words. He followed the hallway as floorboards creaked with each step.

The hallway took a hard right. A black Victorian-style door blocked Jamie's path.

This one did have a lock, resting underneath an ornate handle.

The keyhole looked exactly like the image in the center of the Trusted.Team website.

"No. . . way." Jamie inserted the key, and the door swung right open. A gust of cold air from the darkness danced across his face.

Jamie buttoned up his jacket and stepped forward.

A warm glow of light appeared at the bottom of a worn and weathered stone staircase.

Jamie took each uneven step slowly, using his phone's flashlight and the cold steel handrail as guides.

After thirty or so steps, Jamie reached the lower landing. Three Edison bulbs hung from a low ceiling above yet another door, plain and wooden with an iron knocker.

A crack told Jamie he didn't need to knock. The door swung open easily, its hinges whining.

Jamie gulped and stepped forward.

"The hell?"

The brewpub basement looked nothing like a basement. Three golden chandeliers hung above upholstered furniture, spread across velvety carpet that stretched farther than Jamie could see. Thick curtains and oil paintings adorned the walls.

A figure moved in the shadow of a raven accent chair.

"Hello?" Jamie called out.

Catherine.

"It's you." Jamie strode forward toward the back of the room.

"Yes,"—Catherine nodded, sipping a cup of tea—"so it is."

"Okay, so you can probably imagine how weirded out I am right now." Jamie crossed his arms. "What's with all the. . . the secrecy? And the website and the key and this place? Speaking of which, where the hell are we? I feel like I drove two hours and traveled back two hundred years!"

Catherine set her teacup on a saucer and cracked a smile. "Do you know what the oldest building in New York is, officially?"

"I'm sorry, what?"

"The oldest building in New York City. Officially."

"Uh. . ." Jamie forced a laugh. "If I had to guess. . . maybe that church where Washington got inaugurated. Or retired. Or whatever. Look, I don't know, it's been a few years since I took the tour."

"Nice try, but no," Catherine said. "It's the Wyckoff House. In Brooklyn. Built by a German immigrant and his Dutch wife circa 1650."

"Um, okay. What does that have to do with anything?"

"*Officially*," she said. "The *actual* oldest building was built a bit earlier. 1630."

"Unofficially? Then how would you know?"

"Because we're standing in it."

"Um, what?" Jamie laughed again. "We're standing in it? What exactly is 'it'?"

"The oldest building in New York City. Site of America's first guild. Look around. Why the adornment?" She gestured to the paintings. "The ceiling? Jamie, you're standing in a building the city forgot. Manhattan grew up around this place."

"Okay, okay." Jamie backed away. "I don't mean to be 'that guy,' but you lost me. Like, really lost me. I came here because I was curious. You know, the strategic partner thing?"

"What do you know about guilds?"

"Seriously? I don't care about history. What does any of this have to do with why I left home at three a.m. to drive all the way out here?"

"Perhaps your future needs a lesson in history."

"Look, I've given up half my morning to be here. Cut the crap. Just tell me about this 'Trusted Team' thing before I ask for my fifty bucks back."

"What do you know about guilds?" Catherine repeated, more forcefully this time.

Jamie threw up his hands. "I don't know, okay? I don't know anything about them. A guild is some kind of union or membership group, like the Shiners or Freemasons, right?"

"The guilds were everything people looked for. Everything early workers would've wanted in a network."

"How so?"

"Guilds ruled commerce in Europe for nearly a thousand years. Historically a secret society from which 'networking' groups sprang,"—Catherine took another sip of her tea—"the guilds gave workers a powerful way to collaborate with one another, grow their businesses, and control their own destiny."

"Okay, now you're talking." Jamie slowly took a seat.

"This is the site of the first guild in what would become the United States. These,"—Catherine stepped around her chair and stood over an oblong table—"were the real men who built America. They collaborated inside their industries and between their industries, sharing everything from best practices to customer patron information." Her gaze fell on a piece of crimson velvet laid over something on the table.

"What's that?" Jamie stood and stepped around the deconstructed chair.

"A ledger I wanted to show you," Catherine replied, removing the velvet. "I pulled it from the archives last night."

"Archives?"

Catherine cracked a smile. "Indeed."

The ledger looked like an extremely large and worn old English Bible—a giant leather-bound book with faded writing and thick yellowed pages.

"As far as we know, this is the world's first record of interindustry collaboration and consolidated patron detail. The guilds used these pages to document decades' worth of transactions and track their customers' needs. That way, whenever a building project was commissioned, the guild knew which members to call on, offering nearly unlimited resources. Their process for managing customers and tradesmen was second to none. The feast-or-famine struggle is a modern-day phenomenon. If you got into the guild, you could put food on the table for life."

"Sorry for being a little skeptical, but how do I know any of this is true? I mean, yeah, guilds were real and all, but. . ."

"Fair point. My answer to that question would also explain why you're here."

"What do you mean?" Jamie looked doubtful.

"As the story goes, the guild system collapsed under its own weight. Its exclusivity was a prime feature for centuries, but it eventually became a bug. Guilds dwindled from strategic partnerships into good ole boys' clubs, and their relevance deteriorated. Every networking group on the planet is an echo of the guilds' former glory. Networking is a means for low-level, in-person marketing. These handshake networks are just a cover for a few to make money while the majority of the group provides board memberships and the managing franchise a livelihood. Our Trusted Team exists to restore the significance of strategic partnership and embody the principles that made guilds so successful. After all, the guilds system turned their members into America's first millionaires."

"Isn't that a bit hypocritical? I mean, the whole millionaire thing is great, but you are a major member in the NAB group. Networking is how we met!"

"Nab President Ray has no knowledge of the Trusted Team. Our members are sprinkled in groups like the NAB all over the area to find promising strategic partners. People like you who embody the very principles that made guilds so powerful. So successful. For every member."

"Okay, principles. Please explain. That's what the application said, something about principles. What principles do you think I. . . embody?"

Catherine picked up her tea cup. "The Five Keys of the Trusted Team," she said. "When the guilds lost prominence, the original keys disappeared into history. But we've come together to illuminate new keys to success, supporting a results driven mastermind group of sorts. And you, Jamie, demonstrated the First Key for us last week."

"I did?"

"Yes. 'It's not who you know; it's how you know them.' The referral you received and converted to a sale was the result of both your previous relationship and the new perspective you unveiled in your Network of American Business commercial. You already personally knew LaVell, but judging by his reaction to your expression of how home feels, he was compelled to form a professional relationship with you as well. Your membership with the Trusted Team is pending until you demonstrate the remaining four Keys to us."

"'Us.' You keep saying, 'us' and 'we.' Sounds like Big Brother or something."

"'Us' is other Trusted Team members whom you may or may not have met."

"Whoa." Jamie took a step back. "Like, other people at the Network of American Business? You're all in cahoots?"

"Cahoots?" Catherine smiled. "I guess you could say that. A few of us, yes. The knock you heard Friday was my signal to the others. We're now watching your level of professionalism and ability to contribute with great interest."

"Whoa, back up." Jamie frowned. "I get all this cool history stuff and the book and the Keys, but how is this at all different from regular networking? People pass leads and give referrals there, too. And I don't have to deal with Manhattan rush hour on my way home."

"'Networking.'" Catherine smiled. "Business card swaps are not strategic partnerships. Neither are most referral exchanges. My professional focus helps me track information. An enormous gap exists between 'networking' and how this leather-bound book used to organize tradesmen. We seek to build trust in our clients through effort and consistent results."

"Right. So you're scribing names and addresses in ink on paper ledgers? That's fancy."

"A modern-day equivalent, actually. This is a relic of inefficiency by today's standards, inefficient similar to the Network of American Business referrals passed in carbon copy, triplicate slips. We've evolved to a leads model, defined not by looking out for referrals, but by looking *in* for opportunities for our members, with clients who already know, like, and trust us as subject-matter experts." Catherine sipped her tea and gently put the cup in the saucer.

"I guess I noticed the NAB slips. I didn't really understand the reason for triplicate, though." Jamie eased back into a heavy leather arm chair. "So, can you give me a bit more info about how this team works? I assume that's why I'm here at five a.m."

"Certainly. To get into more detail, let's talk about your professional experience. I find it's easier to explain what we do when I put it into context. Tell me about some of the positions you've held within organizations."

The sound of the upstairs door opening echoed down the staircase, and heavy footsteps followed. Catherine looked toward the basement door.

"Probably checking to see if we'd like anything." She smiled.

Jamie pulled a capped metal pen from his pocket as the bartender slid halfway in the door.

"All good down here?"

"Thank you for checking on us, Lawrence," Catherine said, still smiling. "I'd like some more Earl Grey. Anything for you, Jamie?"

"Um, I never did get that menu," Jamie muttered. He leaned forward stiffly, glancing around. "I'll just have some coffee. Black will work."

The bartender nodded and headed back up the staircase.

"So, let's see, previous jobs. . ." Jamie fiddled with his pen. "I have a pretty varied background from pizza places to construction. Tucker and I worked together at a couple of restaurants, and we bartended together before I left for school. Obviously you know I'm in real estate now."

"All right, let's work backward from where I'm familiar. As a real estate agent, what is your biggest challenge?"

"Well, probably finding people to work with."

"And why is that difficult? Aren't there thousands of people buying and selling homes?"

"Yeah, but I don't know any of them, and certainly none of them know me. I don't exactly have the cash right now to plaster my car with my face or put up a billboard. Do you know how much it costs to put an ad on a hundred grocery carts or buy space for roadside bench ads? I'm starting to get advertising figured out in the NAB, but it isn't easy."

Catherine paused as Lawrence shuffled down the staircase. He pushed the door open with his back, rattling his tray of cups.

"Thank you, Lawrence. Ah, you remembered the lemon. Excellent." Lawrence set down the contents of his tray in front of Catherine and Jamie.

"Anything else I can get you?"

"Not at the moment."

"This works for me, thanks." Jamie grabbed his steaming cup of coffee.

Once Lawrence had left, Catherine continued. "The Network of American Business will be a great start for you to create solid buying relationships. The design of the group is supposed to facilitate referrals and, for your particular focus, drum up some direct prospects. Are you familiar with the process of a one-to-one meeting within the group?"

"Somewhat. It seems sort of like speed dating. I feel like it'll be awkward, but I know I've gotta get out of my comfort zone."

Catherine laughed. "Speed dating? I suppose that's one way to look at it. The concept of a networking group supports professionals by supplying new opportunities. Generally we, as networkers, are working to become known, liked, and trusted. Many groups like the Network of American Business lean on one to ones as a type of currency. The more of these you do, the deeper your professional relationships become."

"Hmm. Okay. So the NAB has a certain process they want us to use for one to ones. Is that how you meet with people?"

"Well, not exactly. My methods are a bit more deliberate. As the NAB focuses on referrals and, let's be candid, one another as prospective customers, I stray from the recommended protocols. My approach or, moreover, *our* approach focuses on leads rather than referrals. Before my one to ones with other NAB members, I'll send a message including the goals of the group and my personal goals. I like transparency, and I clarify what I'm looking for in annual revenue, among other metrics. Some think this is aggressive, while others appreciate my goal-oriented approach."

"I thought the whole point of the NAB was to figure out what we could do for others. Don't take this the wrong way, but your 'approach' sounds kind of selfish."

Catherine paused, slowly moving her tea bag up and down in her fresh cup. "Something you'll hear a lot in networking groups is, 'Let me know if I can help' or 'If there's anything I can do to support you, let me know.' They're advertising good intentions, but I see a wolf in sheep's clothing. My experience over the years has shown me that most of the members offering 'help' and 'support' are really saying, 'Let me know if you want to buy from me' or 'If there's anything I can sell you, let me know.' This type of relationship building feels artificial.

"By stating my goals and value proposition before my one to ones, I offer an example of how I am running my business. This example keeps the one-to-one conversation focused. Whether we discuss my goals first or last, I leave these meetings with a specific understanding of that person's focus and value proposition. I can provide actual support now that I understand the specific needs of those I surround myself with professionally. Most importantly I define a profile of the member's perfect customer, otherwise known as an avatar."

Jamie paused, spinning his pen. "So in your version of networking, you're becoming known by aligning your relationships to your business goals?"

"Professionally, yes."

"Are people open to sharing what they make with you?"

"I don't ask, nor do I care about their annual income. I certainly don't share that information. Here. Let me show you my discovery worksheet." Catherine pulled a sheet of paper from her attaché case. "You see, I've formulated the value proposition, clearly stated my goal for my group membership, and included my origin story. These are the areas that I feel members should understand about one another. By creating a standard, we shore up accountability, while getting to know those with whom we spend time. As you already know, the First Key of the Trusted Team reads, 'It's not who you know; it's how you know them.' By the end of my one to one, I visualize where that member might complement my client base and have a good idea of who they could target."

"So when you say, 'leads not referrals,' you literally mean you offer up your past clients as leads?"

"Certainly. The nature of my relationships is that of a trusted advisor. The people I do business with are all looking for similar products and services. It only makes sense to add value across the board. Many times I have knowledge about my clients' needs outside of what I offer, and usually I've met someone who can provide for that need. Setting up professionals I trust with clients I know need products or services is only logical, wouldn't you agree?"

Jamie leaned his head back. "So if you're doing this in the NAB, why invite me all the way out here to this hidden basement? Don't get me wrong, this is a great one to one, but we could have done this closer to home."

Catherine smiled. "The Network of American Business is just what it says it is, a network. Though I work to be the best member possible, there is little reciprocation."

"Um, didn't you say in your commercial that you were doing business with almost everyone in the NAB?"

"Yes, and I am working with most of the members in some capacity. But my ability to offer expertise generally stops at the members. Seldom does it extend out of the NAB. Networks are not strategic partners. Aligning partnerships is truly about knowing people the right way and having a way to provide value. The Network of American Business *does* provide immediate value but isn't as dynamic as it could be."

Jamie leaned forward, resting his elbows on his knees. "So you think they could be making more money, but NAB members are only capitalizing on other members? Maybe they know you and like you, but do they trust you to sell products or services outside the group?"

"I don't know that they're withholding; I'd just say they're only able to see as far as the NAB supports them. It's a tenured organization with traditional methods. Participation is spurred by rules of reciprocity, peer pressure, and socialization. I am sure you've felt the pressure of passing someone a 'referral' as the meeting closes and others have already added a slip to the pile."

Jamie laughed under his breath. "Yeah, there's definitely some pressure. I thought about referring myself for a message or setting up a planning session with Ray just to contribute."

"We believe the group function is great. That said, we subscribe to the belief that a second sale is always easier than the first. Instead of scribbling out random names on slips of paper, we look into our respective client bases to collaborate. I've already created value for my clients, so why wouldn't I complement my involvement? Keeping records, similar to those in that ledger, helps us curate opportunity with a shared consciousness. By formalizing comradery with Trusted Team members, we can create a broad, deep network of information. Fortunately, we've eclipsed our guild ancestry with modern-day technology. Because information drives exponential growth, our Trusted Team has become the most advanced group of complementary partners I've ever seen or heard of."

"Wait, I'm confused. Network of information? What does that mean?"

"Think about the referral slips the NAB uses."

"Yeah, what about them?"

"Think about the power on each of those slips. If client data is worth more than gold, every time someone identifies a referral opportunity, we *should* be depositing the information into an account somewhere."

Jamie laughed again. "Data is worth more than gold? How is that possible? Are you saying you deposit handwritten slips of paper into a vault or something?"

"Yes, data is worth more than gold. Think of it this way. You have a client who's selling their home and wants to get a property inspection ahead of the go to market. The client asks you if you know an inspector. You, as a Trusted Team member, add a lead to our system for an inspector in your trusted circle. Let's say the inspector goes on-site and notices the roof needs further inspection. As the inspector wraps up his duties, he tells the homeowner that the roof looks like it's toward the end of its life. The home owner agrees and asks for another referral. Since the group is connected via our software system, the inspector is able to schedule an appointment with a Trusted Team roofer on the spot—very convenient for the homeowner—and drops the appointment on the opening in the roofer's calendar. This same scenario could unfold even further past the real estate agent, inspector, roofer, extending to concrete, landscaping, and any complementary trade in this case." Catherine sips her tea.

"Since your client was added to our system, they were discoverable by a multitude of service providers. One name leads to tens of thousands of dollars in commerce. By knowing, liking, and trusting people, a circle of resources is formed that propels each of our professions forward. Like the disparate carbon copy slips used in the NAB, or the old guild ledger containing tradesmen and patron information, our software allows us to concentrate our efforts on gainful professional interaction. Our system is indexed and optimized to support a choose-your-own-client journey."

Jamie was silent for a moment, staring up at the coffered ceiling and fiddling with his pen. "I never thought about something like that. Crazy. I wish I had access to that many possibilities."

"I know it's a lot to take in. But you were invited because we believe you could be a good addition to our team."

"How can I say no to that?" Jamie chuckled. "So can I ask you a question?"

Catherine squeezed the remaining lemon into her teacup. "Absolutely—although I can't guarantee an answer."

"Why me? Aside from me demonstrating your Key, principle thing." He leaned forward, blowing on his cup of coffee.

"Simply put, Jamie, we believe in you. We believe you can add to our symbiotic team relationship, creating more for everyone."

"Wow."

She sat back in her chair, legs crossed under her long white suit skirt. "Now, let's talk about your friend, Tucker."

"Oh. Okay. What about Tucker?"

"He is your friend, correct?"

"Well, yeah. Is Tucker invited, too?"

"How do you know him?"

"How do I know Tucker? Uh. . . we met in high school. We were at college together for a while, too. He's a friend, even though he's kind of the used-car-salesman type. Which is exactly what he does. Ironic, right?"

"But you're not that type."

"No, at least, I don't think so." Jamie waited for a reply, which he didn't get. "Should I be?"

"LaVell was Tucker's customer before he became your referral, wasn't he?"

"Uh. . . I wouldn't call him Tucker's customer. Prospect, definitely. Is that what you're asking?"

"It is, yes. Here is my offer." Catherine stood, buttoned her jacket, and purposefully slid on tight, brown leather gloves. "You, myself, and Tucker. A group one to one. If you can schedule that, we will talk some about what else is on our team-membership horizon. The time is getting on, so I need to be off." She stretched out a gloved hand.

Jamie swallowed. "Deal."

"Lawrence has been taken care of. Be sure you give him back the key when you leave."

"I'll walk out with you. I'm about finished."

"No, no. Enjoy the coffee. Think a bit, and be sure to lock up. Wouldn't want any uninviteds to discover our meeting hall."

Chapter 5

Jamie opened a new text and started typing.

"Hey, so I followed up with Catherine. Wanted to know more about the biz card. Set up a group 1:1 so we can ask her. Tomorrow @ lunch. Does that work for you?"

Tucker replied.

"You mean a threesome? High fives only LOL. Nice going. I got some questions for her. Send me addy. Meet you in parking lot 5 min before."

Jamie walked uphill toward the country club from the back of the parking lot. A small cloud of smoke hovered under the awning at the entrance.

Tucker.

"Jamie!" Tucker called out. He coughed and flicked his cigarette into the bushes.

"Hey, what's up?" Jamie climbed the brick steps. He closed his umbrella.

"All right, I've been scoping this place out. Catherine's here already. Bar and grill right next to the first tee box." Tucker stepped closer to Jamie and lowered his voice.

"Kinda ritzy and old school. More my thing." He pointed to himself thumb to chest and stuck up his chin. "I can see why she wanted to meet me here."

"Actually, I suggested this place."

"Ha! Sure." Tucker scratched the razor burn showing above his blue oxford collar. "Half a shot of whiskey here, and there goes all your commission. The good whiskey. How much did I let you make off LaVell again?"

"Dude, old news." Jamie smiled at a senior golfer shuffling past them to the door. "You said you wanted to meet a few minutes early."

"Right." Tucker stepped between Jamie and the door. "You don't know how one to ones work. You didn't happen to bring your networking sheet from NAB, did you?"

"My what?"

"'Course not."

"Don't see you holding one." Jamie motioned at Tucker.

Tucker's eyes rolled. "You think I need that entry-level bullshit? I've been a member for months. Now, listen. Catherine's got class. If I'm gonna have a chance with her, I need you to follow my lead."

"Tuck—"

Tucker spun around and dramatically shoved both entry doors open as he attempted his grand entrance into the lobby.

"Wanna tone down the theatrics, Count of Monte Cristo?" Jamie muttered.

Tucker marched past the host stand in the marble hall and made a beeline for the bar.

"Our party's already seated, thanks," Jamie said to the host.

Mounted heads of American wildlife lined the restaurant walls. Catherine sat at a table overlooking a putting green, just below a stag. An open laptop held her gaze.

Jamie followed Tucker to Catherine's table. She looked up when Jamie reached for the chair opposite her.

"Catherine, hola!" Tucker's outside voice boomed.

She smiled quietly. "Hello, gentlemen. Please, join me."

Tucker yanked out the chair opposite Catherine, forcing Jamie back. "Dude, sit. Don't be rude," he said to Jamie as he confidently crossed his legs leaning back into the chair. He waved at the server. "Menus please, and a whiskey, neat." He turned back to Catherine. "So, how's life? You look busy."

"Productive, not busy. Pardon me one more sec." Catherine silenced her buzzing phone and resumed typing. "Just finishing an email."

"No problem," Jamie said. "Good to see you again— good to see you."

Catherine's eyes met Jamie's, her fingers still typing away. "Nice to see you as well, Jamie."

The server, wiry with a thin moustache, approached with Tucker's drink and handed menus to Tucker and Jamie.

"For you, monsieur?" he said to Tucker.

Tucker handed the menu right back. "*Je veux du steak bien cuit.*"

The server scribbled his order onto a notepad. "*Et vous, monsieur?*"

"Me?" Jamie chuckled. "Um. . ." He scanned the appetizers. "Just some cinnamon raisin toast, please. I had a big breakfast."

"Very well." The server raised an eyebrow at Catherine.

"Another cup, please." She held up a ceramic cup.

"Still drinking coffee this late?" Tucker said.

"Tea, wasn't it?" Jamie said. A squeezed tea bag left a stain on Catherine's plate.

"Observant." Catherine winked at Jamie.

"Caffeine's caffeine." Tucker leaned forward as he scooted his chair closer to the table. "So I've gotta be honest with you, Cath. I'm in the group all this time, trying to set up a meeting with you, and this rookie here,"—Tucker mussed Jamie's hair—"gets an appointment with you right off the bat. Don't get me wrong, I'm glad you and I are finally sitting down. But it sends a guy the message you might be playing hard to get." Tucker leaned back and sipped his whiskey. "If you know what I mean."

Catherine watched her laptop. "I keep my one to ones strictly professional. Why don't you tell me a little bit about what you do? Professionally."

"Uh," Tucker laughed, "exactly what you hear me say every Friday?"

"Yes, I know you work at a Cadillac dealership. What I'm curious about is how you conduct your business."

"Oh, sure. I get it." Tucker crossed his arms, still holding his drink. "I've got some questions for you, too. I typically like receiving first, but either way." He winked again. "So as you know, I sell cars. But what I really do is make guys feel like a million bucks by getting them in the chariot of their dreams. And I make a lot of dreams come true, let me tell you."

"I can vouch for that," Jamie said. "He averages, what, eighteen cars a month?"

"Damn right. I've only been there for sixteen months, and I've been the monthly volume sales leader ten times." Tucker leaned in. "Ten. Times."

"How many times?" Catherine inquired, raising her eyebrows with a smile. "So, at the dealership, do you manage relationships with customers or just sell, sell, sell?"

"Nice try, Cath. Trick question. They're the same thing. A lot of people don't get that a relationship is a sale. There are easier transactional relationships, like hooking up with the intern." He gave her yet another wink. "And there are developing relationships like ours. Either way, we all want the same thing: to score something that makes us feel good, something we can walk away with feeling satisfied."

Catherine picked up her phone and typed something with her thumb.

"What I think Tucker means," Jamie said quickly, "is that he focuses on the drives of his clients and works hard to develop both short- and long-term prospective relationships somehow. Right?"

"*Psh*. Dude, no. I said what I meant. What's there to work at? Either I sell you your dream car, or you don't have the money. I work for a thumbs-up or the middle finger."

"Clearly you have a handle on your dealings. Zig Ziglar reincarnate." Catherine motioned her cup in a faux cheers.

The server slid Jamie's toast onto the table.

"Hey, how long for that steak?" Tucker asked. "You're supposed to bring everybody's meals at once."

"My apologies, monsieur. Just a few more minutes on the steak. If you like I can. . ." The server motioned to Jamie's plate.

"No, thank you. This is fine. You can leave my toast." Jamie picked up his napkin.

"Very well." The server hurried off.

"Tucker, you seem prolific. I trust your employer compensates you accordingly?"

"Ha, I wish!" Tucker whipped out his phone. "You wanna say that again? I'll record you and show my boss."

"Perhaps not." Catherine sipped her tea. "I take it you don't use any type of contact manager or account management systems?"

"No, we use a dealer track. It does a lot of the same things." Jamie's eyes shot up to Catherine's. She smiled. "Anyway, I'm all about pounding the pavement, getting the word out, and wheeling and dealing. That's how I set all these records. And that's why I'm in the NAB. To move as many cars off my floor as fast as possible."

"Confident." Catherine nodded slowly. "You are in the right business. Salespeople need confidence. So these months with the Network of American Business, I can assume you've sold some vehicles to group members? Have you had any opportunity to sell multiple cars to anyone?"

"I've had a his-and-hers deal with Ray. His wifey got a hell of a deal on her Escalade. Typical female. I had to set up all her navigation and hands-free security crap. I'm always following up, trying to hook the friends and family." Tucker cut into his steak as the server stood at attention. "*Beauté. Je vous remercie.*"

"Sounds service-oriented. Are you working to build a good contact list for your future?"

"Look, Cath, I am your guy for cars." Tucker talked through a cheek full of steak. "New, used, domestic, import. I get it. You're trying to follow the NAB rule book. Let's just cut through all this and get to the point. You know what I do. How I do it isn't really relevant. Trade secrets, you know?"

"Fair enough." Catherine sipped. "I can appreciate your zest and ability to play the part in your profession. As much as I would love to hear more about your profession and how you are the embodiment of an alpha, I really need some grounds to relate my profession. I do not have the luxury others are provided when it comes to my work. My goal regarding this meeting was to acquaint myself with you gentlemen and facilitate a clearer understanding of one another. Ultimately, everyone should be given the opportunity to be known, liked, and trusted. Without an understanding of infrastructure, leading to your self-advertised success, I will struggle to conceptualize my work for you. That said, perhaps Mr. Morris can help illuminate my dealings. "Now, Jamie." She shifted in her chair, crossing her legs toward him. "How is it you do what you do?"

Jamie looked at Tucker, leaning forward toward Catherine. "Should I use that networking sheet? Or. . ."

"Authentic Networking Objectives and Assignments sheet? I believe Ray phased that out a couple of months ago. Didn't he, Tucker?" Catherine said without losing focus on Jamie.

"I don't remember him saying that. Jamie, dude, don't worry about it. We'll just chalk this meeting up to practice. You're still learning."

"Sure." Jamie cleared his throat. "Well, maybe it's 'cause I'm a 'rookie,'" he said, putting the last word in air quotes. "But I'm more of a relationships guy. I'd rather get a feeling for a client's wants and needs before they buy a home. I mean, before they purchase a home with me. That's kind of what brought me to the Network of American Business, actually. I wasn't having much luck passing out business cards, and the group seemed like a good opportunity to show up, build relationships, and create some value."

"I like that philosophy." Catherine sipped her tea. "Go on."

"Well, consider the source here," Tucker butted in. "Jamie's sold only one house before. I'm over at the dealership setting records. No one there has ever been rewarded three all-expenses-paid company trips, and I've been on three this year alone."

"Congratulations," Catherine said, deadpan. "I'm glad you had it in your heart to invite Jamie to the networking group. After all, we really needed a real estate agent, someone with the right potential and the right attitude. We have a lot of assets in the group who can complement your business, Jamie: handymen, HVAC techs, roofers. All ideal contacts for you. You haven't mentioned how you got into real estate."

"Oh. Well, I got my license from a business college, but I really got my start with my dad."

"At least you got something out of college," Tucker interjected before throwing back the remaining whiskey from his glass.

"Interesting." Catherine kept her gaze on Jamie. "How is it the two of you know each other, exactly?"

"Tucker and I went to high school together." Jamie gave more detail this time. "And we worked at the same restaurant. Then we were roommates for a while when I was in community college. There's a group of us who all kinda grew up together. That's also how we know LaVell."

"Look, whether we're talking sales or chicks, I've taught him everything he knows," Tucker professed. "In fact, I bet that's how he was able to swing all of us getting together today. Probably a pickup line I gave him." Tucker rolled his eyes. "So unprofessional, Jamie."

"What's your deal today?"

"Relax, man." Tucker turned to Catherine. "Guy can't take a joke. Or handle a bet. I passed the three-bill thrill this month. That's three hundred thousand in sales, and it's not even—"

"Look, I have to go." Jamie pushed back his now-cold toast. "Sorry. I've. . . I. . . I'm getting a phone call." He pulled out his phone, hiding the lock screen from Catherine and Tucker. "I'm sorry, this person is a client." He tossed a wadded-up ten-dollar bill at his food. "That should cover it. Sorry, Catherine." Jamie hurried toward the door.

"Geez, can you believe that guy? I was just joking. Kid's got a lot to learn. Just sit down, Jamie!" he belted over his shoulder. "The call can wait! We're just getting into the good stuff." Tucker waved his empty glass at the approaching server. "Hey, how 'bout on the rocks this time? It's a celebration!" He turned back to Catherine. "I am *killing* it this year. He's so screwed. I don't know what all he's told you, but that first sale he bragged about? That was all me. I set him up with LaVell. I'll keep setting him up 'cause I love him like a brother. But he doesn't stand a chance of closing more deals than me."

Catherine said nothing.

"How 'bout some mimosas?"

"No, thank you. So, let me ask you a question." Catherine shifted her posture toward Tucker.

"Shoot."

"Why did you bring Jamie to the group?"

"Exactly what you said. We needed a real estate agent with the right attitude and some potential. After that little retreat, I'm not sure about the attitude part."

"I think you did a good job with Jamie. Perhaps he's about to close his second sale."

"Oh, please. You had to see through that fake call." Tucker pointed at the empty chair. "Like I said, he's a newbie at this networking thing. Doesn't deal well with pressure."

"We shall see." Catherine politely motioned to the server. "Before I wrap up a one to one, I like to see if I can be of service. Is there anything I can help you with, Tucker?"

Tucker grinned. "On the record or off?"

"You've obviously misunderstood today's exchange, Tucker."

"If you say so." Tucker finished his last bite of steak. "Tell you what. I think I've got the perfect car for you. Been thinking about it ever since I saw that little number you're in. What's your current monthly on that? Somebody selling tens of millions a year should be in something way more classy."

"Selling tens of millions?" Catherine smiled, squinting an eyebrow up. "What makes you say that?"

"You don't gotta beat around the bush with me, Cath. Everybody knows," Tucker said. "Jamie told me. He told everybody."

"Is—Is that so? Really?"

Tucker leaned closer. "If I'm not mistaken, the Network of American Business has a rule about their members not being allowed to join other networking groups. What happens if someone is moonlighting on the Network of American Business with another group? Could do some real damage to a person's reputation."

"It certainly could. Have you heard of someone working in another group aside from ours?"

"Nobody in particular. Not directly. Just saying." Tucker flicked his credit card onto the server's bill. "Don't worry about your tea. I can get it for you."

"No need, Tucker. You can place that card back in your pocket. I've already signed for lunch. Credit cards are not accepted here. My apologies, I didn't mean to distract from your nice little story. What were you saying?" Catherine stood and picked up her laptop bag.

"That you should've given me this." From his wallet, Tucker pulled out the black Trusted Team card. "Not Jamie. *Me*. If there's anybody who fits the description 'next valuable asset' for your Trusted-dot-Team, you're looking at him. Remember that."

"I'm not sure I understand what you're referring to."

"Then Ray won't either. I hope."

Catherine took a step toward Tucker, towering over him. "I'm quite sure I'll have to plead ignorance on this. Now I have another appointment. Perhaps if you have any other questions for me, we can discuss them next Friday." With that, she walked off.

"Everything all right, monsieur?" the server came up and asked.

"Perfect. Thank you." Tucker cleared his throat. "Actually, I'll have another." He held up his empty glass, rattling around the half-melted ice ball. "Your best whiskey. It's a celebration, remember?"

The server nodded and headed to the bar. Tucker typed a message to Jamie.

"Catherine is pissed. Says, 'That was so unprofessional. I shouldn't have invited him to my team.' IDK what you should do. I tried patching things up between you guys."

Tucker stepped onto the patio for a smoke and waited for a reply. Jamie didn't respond. Tucker sent another text.

"Don't be too hard on yourself. Everyone screws up."

No reply. Another.

"Ghosting me, huh? Whatev, dude. C u Friday."

Still nothing.

"Worst threesome ever. So much potential!"

Chapter 6

"I've got a check for you," Jamie said.

"Fantastic." Ray smiled. "We're really excited to have you as a member."

"Yeah? I mean,"—Jamie shifted side to side—"I really like this group. I think I've gotten some traction." He waved at LaVell, who balanced a cup of coffee and two donuts on a plate. LaVell nodded back.

"It was Tucker who invited you, right?"

"Yeah, it was."

"Okay, perfect." Ray scribbled something on a clipboard.

"Here's everything." Jamie laid a manila envelope down on the check-in table. "Application, check and all."

"Hey!" a voice from behind Jamie said. "Just make sure that check doesn't bounce."

Tucker.

Jamie stared down at the table.

"Jamie." Ray chuckled. "Should I listen to your friend?"

"Some friend," Jamie muttered under his breath.

"Dude, what gives? Why haven't you texted me back?" Tucker stepped out of line and joined Ray behind the table. "Hey, Mr. El Prezidento."

"Oh, you texted me?" Jamie said in a high-pitched voice. "Wow, tum. . ." He pulled out his phone. "I guess I've just been so busy the past couple of days with LaVell and Cornell and their closing and everything."

"And that new lead."

"New lead? What new lead?"

Tucker shook his head. "Never mind. So,"—he gave a friendly slap to the president's shoulder—"it's official then. The real estate agent category is finally filled. We sure are glad you didn't choose to join that other networking group."

Ray pulled away from the networker checking in next to Jamie and raised his eyebrows. "Other networking group? Which other group had your attention?"

"Yeah, Jamie, tell him about that other group. I thought you were gonna join that one instead."

Ray slid Jamie's application back toward him, slowly. "I hate to break out the rulebook, but our members are allowed only one networking group membership. Ours or someone else's."

"No, no, there's—I'm not—ugh." Jamie sighed. "Look, there is no other group. I'm not joining any other networking group." He glanced at the guest beside him, who immediately looked away. "I'm all in here, okay? I've really been looking forward to officially joining. I'm not interested in a different group."

"Okay, glad we're clear on that, phew." Ray wiped pretend sweat from his brow. "I'll see you both inside. We're backing up here." Ray leaned around to look at the check-in line behind Jamie.

"Sorry, yeah. Thanks," Jamie said. "We're all—we're all good."

Tucker punched Jamie's arm. "Dude! I know you've been getting my messages." He followed Jamie toward the breakfast table. "You've got a serious problem with Catherine. That could've been so much worse if I hadn't—"

"I get it!"

The startled plumber ahead of them in line spilled his coffee.

"Oh gosh, I'm sorry," Jamie stammered.

The plumber's walrus mustache twitched. His trucker cap sat low on his head, hiding his eyes.

"Sorry, again. . ." Jamie turned back to Tucker. "Look, you were right, okay? It's probably a scam. It's all a scam. I don't know what I was thinking giving her fifty bucks, let alone paying triple what it costs to join the NAB."

Tucker nodded. "Yeah. Hey, it could happen to anyone," he said in a fatherly tone. "It wasn't your fault."

"Of course it was." Jamie mashed the coffee machine lever. He filled his Styrofoam cup to the brim. "She should've picked you anyway."

"Yeah, you're right,"—Tucker snatched artificial sweetener packets—"but hey, lesson learned."

"Yep. You go ahead. I think I'm gonna go sit over by, um. . ." Jamie scanned the room. Networkers stood chatting in groups of two or three, or sat shoveling eggs and bacon into their mouths alone.

Except for one—

Catherine.

She stood in the conference room doorway, staring at Jamie, motionless, expressionless—like she'd been there for more than a few seconds.

Jamie didn't finish his thought. He ducked into a conversation triangle of insurance agents.

"Hey, fellas," he said. Chatter burst into laughter— someone dropped a punchline to a joke, something about someone's wife. Jamie backed away to sip his coffee in solitude.

But there she was. Catherine. Headed right toward him.

No escaping the awkwardness now.

"Well, hi!" Jamie waved once she reached handshake distance.

Catherine kept eye contact but said nothing.

"So, how was the rest of lunch the other day? You and Tucker have a good talk?"

"Yes, we did. I'm just sorry you had to leave early. I hope your call went well." Finally, a hint of a smile. "You put your application in here today, I saw."

"Yeah. Spying on me?" He laughed. "But no, it's a great group of people. I guess since I'm not going to work out for your group I should stick with what works, you know?"

Catherine lowered her voice. "Not work out for Trusted Team? What makes you say that?"

"Um, I thought that's what. . . I thought that's what you wanted to say to me. Like, that's the reason we're talking right now. Isn't it?"

"Absolutely not." Catherine emphasized each consonant. "I wanted to give you this." She held out an NAB networking slip.

"A—a referral?"

"Yes. I've decided to sell my house, and this referral is for you."

"Seriously?" Jamie jumped as Tucker appeared behind them. "Why didn't you say anything at our threesome?"

"Excuse me?" Catherine stared at Tucker, eyes tight.

"Lunch." Tucker raised an eyebrow. "The other day? Remember?"

"Yes. Well, I've finally settled on the right property. It's a fixer-upper, but nothing a team of professionals can't handle. Jamie, have you worked with contractors for renovations before?"

"Ha! The guy's sold like, what, one-and-a-half houses?" Tucker gulped his coffee and immediately spit it back into his cup, burning his tongue.

Jamie rolled his eyes.

"Think you can handle it, Jamie?"

"Sure, yeah. I can give it my best. Do you already have contractors picked out? I know there's a plumber. . ." Jamie looked around, scanning the room.

"You might say that. I'll need help with both selling my current house and closing on my new property. Do you have time in your schedule for a high-maintenance client?" Catherine smiled.

"Hey," Tucker said, "whatever you guys work out sounds great, but don't you think I deserve some credit here? What's that category we use, 'thank you for closed business off a referral,' or something like that?"

"Do you think I should give you credit?" Catherine gave Tucker a once-over with her eyes.

"I introduced you guys."

"The meeting is about to start," Jamie said quickly. "Let's talk later."

"Tucker, give us a minute, will you?"

Tucker smiled at Catherine. She didn't reciprocate.

"Whatever. Have your little secrets. Just don't forget about the Cadillac man. Not too much to ask around here." He pulled out a cigarette and lighter from his jacket and walked out.

"That was uncomfortable," Jamie said once Tucker disappeared through the conference-room doorway. "Should we get a seat or—"

"Yes, but quickly." Catherine lowered her purse off her shoulder. "I am eager for you to take another step into our little world. I have a teammate, so to speak, who is key in our project. As I detailed, my colleagues are instrumental in opportunities from the guild perspective."

"You're really still good with me on this whole thing?"

"Yes. I believe Mr. Gerhard will be somewhat of a beacon in the dark for you. A bit more of a hands-on engagement may serve your purpose."

Ray finger-whistled to quiet the room.

"I'll connect the two of you. He'll be the tradesman for my upcoming renovations. Mr. William Joseph." Catherine's voice lowered. She motioned to an empty table. "William Joseph Gerhard."

"Okay, great. Should we all meet or—"

"I'll set you up now." She sat down and pulled out her phone. "Then you can take it from there. And it is 'William Joseph,' not William or Will."

"Or Billy Joe?" Jamie joked.

Catherine didn't laugh.

"Sorry." Jamie pulled out the folding chair next to Catherine.

Ray launched into his speech—a referral group, not a social group, all about ROI, with every referral tracked.

Jamie's phone buzzed.

Again.

Then again.

And again.

The insurance agents' table glared at him.

"Sorry, forgot to—" Jamie fumbled through his pocket for his phone. It wasn't a phone call. A text message, an email, and messages to every social media profile.

"Jamie: /One has connected you with /Two. Type 'View Contact' to see the trusted member profile of. . ."

A second text appeared. And email. And messages.

"William Joseph Gerhard."

Chapter 7

"Whoa," Jamie said under his breath.

He rounded the circular driveway, parking between the weed-infested fountain and the substantial stone porch. An awning stood two stories high on top of four white Doric columns. Ivy crept up the front of the mansion, hiding the second-story windows. Overgrown bushes hid the first floors—if there even were windows. Passersby couldn't tell either way.

"Looks kinda like the White House. After the apocalypse."

Jamie grabbed the folder of home appraisal documents he'd printed off at the library after the NAB meeting and strode up the steps. Cloudy glass panels bordering the double doors offered no glimpse inside.

"Hello? William Joseph?" he called as he knocked lightly. "Are you here?"

Footsteps. Loud, creaky ones. Shuffling. The right door called a squeal as Jamie opened it.

"Um, hello?" Jamie said again.

Out of an unsettled dust cloud stepped a long-haired man in his fifties, wearing leather suspenders, a leather bracelet, and a leather tool belt to match.

"Mr. Jamie Morris, Ms. Catherine Hawthorn's real estate contact, I presume?" He planted his hands on his hips.

"Yeah, and you must be her contractor. William Joseph, right?"

"Indeed I am." William Joseph hopped down off the elevated entryway to the porch and bowed slightly from the waist. A tiny anvil on his necklace peeked out of his shirt, along with more hair. "William Joseph Gerhard, pleased to meet you." He took a half step back and extended an open hand. "I think of myself as more of a master carpenter than a general contractor."

"Cool." Jamie accepted the handshake. "Well, I don't usually bow when I greet people." He laughed awkwardly. "So I guess you. . . found the place unlocked?"

"*Found* it unlocked?" William Joseph let out a low chuckle and scratched his beard. "Yes, let's go with that." He stepped to one side and swept out an arm while tucking the other behind his back. "After you, fine sir."

Jamie entered. A chipped gold chandelier reduced to a mangled knot sat at the base of a grand staircase, blocking access to the kitchen.

"Man, Catherine wasn't kidding. Really is a fixer-upper."

"Disrepair is always regrettable, but it's nothing two skilled hands and some ingenuity can't fix. Ms. Hawthorn needs me to breathe new life into the bones of this chateau." William blew a heavy breath across his open hand. "Add travertine to the bathroom, build a full bath here on the first floor, install new kitchen counters, and knock out a wall to make a master suite out of the guest quarters and the study."

"You can do all that? Geez, that's a lot of work. Catherine must be paying you a bundle. I guess I always thought carpenters made shelves and cabinets and stuff."

William Joseph scratched at his neck, either his beard or his hair. There was so much of both. "We're a bit more advanced than television shows would reveal. I estimate twenty-four days of labor, no more. We must be wise with our time. We have none to waste!" He clapped his open leathery palms together. "I've already strolled the site and got what I need. You'll probably want a tour yourself."

"Right." Jamie opened his folder. "I need to look at a few things and get your ideas on maybe a fair market value to offer the city. I'm guessing at least twenty or twenty-five percent less than the last sale price."

"One million, fifty thousand, seven hundred dollars." William Joseph nodded. "I do my homework, too."

"Right, so three-quarters of a million. Somewhere in that ballpark. Fair market value. It's kind of a wreck." Jamie peeked into the first room on the left: a dim, dilapidated library where a ladder with casters leaned against empty bookshelves. An oversize chair wrapped in a white dust protector sheet faced a looming window. "And a little creepy."

"Ah, but it smells like history." He inhaled, filling his barrel chest with air. "A 1922 build with five bedrooms." William Joseph strained to stare up at the cobwebbed ceiling. "A whole family of Gatsby's may have grown from infant to adulthood here."

"Of who? Never heard of them. But anyway, I've got this renovations checklist, and I know Catherine wants a precise rundown of the costs."

"Got your quote right here." William Joseph pulled a sealed envelope out of his rucksack. "I've included product and labor costs for each repair. Ms. Hawthorn already has a copy. But feel free to take a walk about the place. Appraisers appraise."

"I'm not really an appraiser but, uh, thanks. Thanks a lot, actually. I mean. . ." Jamie tucked the envelope into his folder. "That was like, eighty percent of the reason I came here. To calculate repairs and expenses and stuff. See the place in person."

"So, what was the other twenty percent?"

"Well, um. . ." Jamie glanced at the door. "I got your message. Through. . . the team system."

"The Trusted Team."

"Yeah, that."

William Joseph folded his arms over his chest. His biceps were the size of most men's legs. "Ms. Hawthorn hasn't made a certain point clear to you yet. That's why you and I were to meet."

"Oh. Well. She said you'd help me understand some things, and she said you were working on this project."

"So was she referencing you as the project or the Gatsby château?"

"Uh, well. . ."

"Either way, we've taken this residence as far as possible today. Now let me comment on evolving. It's come to the attention of the Prospect Committee that certain applicants would be wise to augment their personal associations, as future professional success could be influenced."

Jamie gave a nervous laugh. "What the hell does that mean? Not very clear if you ask me."

"Touché. Let me start at the beginning. You know of the Five Keys. Your ability to manifest them in your behavior determines your acceptance. Is this something you recall? Something familiar?"

"Keys? Oh, right, right. 'It's not your friends, but how you know them.' That was numero uno." Jamie held up a finger.

"Not the best Spanish or the best memory. 'It's not who you know but how you know them' is how the Key reads. But yes, you're right, that is the First Key to unlocking your future. You've partially exemplified that one already. Started to prove yourself. It's the remaining ones we want to explore a bit."

"Look, Mr. Gerhard."

"You may call me William Joseph."

"I am not the note-taking kind," Jamie said. "The conversation Catherine and I had in the city came at me a million miles an hour. Kind of a whirlwind."

"I see. Well, our Trusted Team is built on the foundational Five Keys. The first is as you referenced it, 'It's not who you know but how you them." The second, 'Setup is always better than follow-up.' The third, 'Information drives exponential growth.' The fourth, 'The second sale is always easier than the first.'"

"Wait, this is too much too fas—"

"That's how the Fourth Key reads," William Joseph interrupted. "The Trusted Team realizes most of the work is done building up the initial opportunity. Past that, creating secondary opportunities should come much easier. But I digress. Before we drill down on Keys two, three, and four, the fifth, accountability, goes both ways and caps off our binding principles."

Jamie pushed to finish his thought. "I wasn't objecting to the fourth principle, keybinder thing, whatever. This is just a lot to take in. It's a ton of information and seems like some standards I just can't. . ."

"Mr. Morris, these are not so complicated as to cause distress. Could be I took you literally, starting down the list as a way to illuminate our canon. All things considered, we really should tune to that initial key, as it were. We expect discernment in your relationships. In whom you put your trust informs the careful observer whether or not they can trust you. For you this is a double-edged sword."

"I feel like you're trying to give me some sort of a hint."

"As you impressed Catherine, evolving before her very eyes, it seems you've an anchor holding your ship in its port of origin. Release yourself from the past. Set sail. Form alliances with only the worthy."

"Wait a second. This isn't about Tucker, is it?"

"Ms. Hawthorn gave me no names. She voiced concern about one association and its negative influence. Your ties to individuals past and future determine your success. Strategic partnerships require absolute trust on each side. Can you honestly say you absolutely depend on all of your current acquaintances?"

"Look, maybe you are talking about Tucker. I don't know. Tucker's just a guy I've known for a long time. Simply a friend."

"*What?*" William Joseph gnashed his teeth. "Never, *ever* use the word *just*. It delivers the exact opposite message you intended. And in conjunction with *simply*, no less. Nothing is ever *just*, *simply*. These terms minimize. Dilute. And distract. Words, like action, matter, Mr. Morris."

"Okay. All right. You made your point. I'm sorry. Geez. You've gotta admit, you're being a little weird about all of this."

"Why? Is our secret society code too discerning for you?"

"I just—I mean, I feel like every time I talk to you guys, I go around in circles. First the card. Then that website puzzle and meeting Catherine in some secret ancient basement. Or whatever. That whole place was like something out of a movie. I'm still not sure I believe the whole forgone guild story. All I had to do to join the NAB group was hand over a check. With you guys, I can't seem to get a complete answer to anything! Don't get me wrong. Catherine seems like a powerhouse. She knows her stuff. I just don't—I mean, if these Five Keys matter so much, why has it taken so long to explain them to me? And how the hell do I embody all of them, or whatever you call it? Am I being graded right now? See? I have no clue."

"Every group has its fundamental beliefs. Freemasons. Catholics. Pagans. The high school glee club. We, the Trusted Team, believe that our five core principles, when abided by in the context of strategic partnerships, multiply efforts more consistently than any other approach to business development. I wouldn't be part of the group if it didn't pay dividends. But it does. I haven't invested one shekel promoting my business since I joined. I don't even have a sign or a website. Why would I need one? All the exposure I need, my Trusted Team provides."

"Good for you. Hope it continues to work out. All I'm saying is, it sure would be nice to know how I'm supposed to pass your Five Key test thing. A study guide would be nice."

"All right, Mr. Morris. Again. One." William Joseph raised a finger. "'It is not who you know; it is how they are known.' Two." He raised two fingers. "'Setup is far better than follow-up.' Three, 'Information drives exponential growth.' Four, 'The second sale is always easier than the first.' And five, 'Accountability goes both ways.'"

"Can I. . ." Jamie uncapped his pen and scribbled on the back of his folder. "Can I get a copy of all that? It's a lot to remember."

"Indeed they are. In due time, Mr. Morris. Have I clarified any of this for you?"

"Um, no? You didn't answer my question about exemplifying all of them."

"Let me put this plainly," William Joseph said. "Trusted or steerage. It is not a test; this is a matter of perception. Understanding with some perspective helps one see true value."

"Not a test, huh? Then why do I feel like I am being tutored all of a sudden? Why help me with Catherine? Why go to the trouble of doing all the heavy lifting on the remodeling estimates? While you're listing keys and offering enlightenment and teaching philosophy, maybe you can write me out some flash cards next."

William Joseph smiled. "As I say, indeed. In due time. Your takeaway today should absolutely be, 'It's not who you know; it's how you know them.' Before this conversation, I didn't know you. I didn't know anything about you. Except for the fact Catherine respects you. That's how I know you. All I am asking you is, can you say the same of all your strategic partners?"

"I don't have any strategic partners. Well, not until this Trusted Team deal."

William Joseph side-eyed him—the same way Catherine did. "I wouldn't be too sure about that."

"Well, if you'll excuse me, I've got a tour to take. And a home to sell and a house to buy."

"Godspeed, Mr. Jamie Morris," William Joseph said, stretching out for a tight handshake. "Don't worry about locking up. I shall return this fine day. Good fortune!"

"Sounds good. Have a good day."

Alone, Jamie tore open the envelope. He pulled out a one-page quote with company letterhead—"Gerhard & Company"—and tight cursive handwriting that was as legible as the US Constitution. At least the numbers stood out. Line-item estimates were written for every repair, each with its corresponding damage, calculating Catherine's first offer.

"Trusted Team or not, ten more Catherines, and I'm retired," he whispered. He stepped into the library for a self-guided tour and some reflection.

Chapter 8

"Catherine?" Jamie said quietly.

"Oh, good morning." She turned from her place in the breakfast line. "I didn't see you there."

"Morning." Jamie shifted. "So yeah, I met with, uh. . ." He exchanged glances with the networkers in line on either side of Catherine. "You know."

"I know." She smiled and nodded. "He spoke highly of you. William Joseph 'rendered you someone to know.'"

"Really? Okay. I mean, great. Thanks. So anyway, we put this offer together for you." Jamie pulled a folder out of his messenger bag. "Are you available to talk right after the NAB meeting or—"

"Jamie!"

Tucker sputtered and stumbled into the room, tripping over the leg of the first chair he passed. He awkwardly caught himself on an adjacent table, shaking the four networkers' coffee cups. His blue button-down shirt was half untucked, a beer stain covering the front of it. Cigarettes flew out of his pocket.

"Ow!"

Everyone let out a collective gasp.

"Tucker, oh my God!" Jamie rushed across the room and grabbed Tucker's arm. "Tucker, you good, man? Geez, are you. . . are you *drunk?*"

Tucker rocked a bit, trying to straighten himself up. "Jamie, I gotta tell ya, man. . ." Tucker lost his balance again, and grabbed the chair. "You screwed up. You screwed up, dude. You screwed me over." He reached out with both hands to scoop up his cigarettes but tumbled forward.

"Get a whiff of that? This kid is wasted," a nearby networker whispered to LaVell.

"You were s'posed to be my friend, dude," Tucker continued from the floor, "and you leave me hanging for Catherine! You think she's better than me? That woman—"

"Okay, you're drunk." Jamie pulled away. "Not a good look for you. You shouldn't be here like this."

Ray appeared in the doorway as Tucker pulled himself off the floor.

"What's going on? I heard a—Tucker, what. . ." Ray stopped, looking at Tucker's fistful of bent and broken cigarettes.

"Tucker needed. . ." Jamie began, but stopped midsentence.

Tucker shoved the cigarettes back in his pocket and snickered.

"Oh my." Ray put his arms out to the gathering crowd around Tucker. "Let's handle this professionally, now."

"Tucker, let's go to my car," Jamie said, extending his hand to Tucker. Jamie lowered his voice. "Come on, man, we gotta get you outta here. You're making a fool out of yourself. They're going to throw you out."

"You aren't going to win. You'll never catch up to me." Tucker's words slurred under his breath. He spun around, grabbing a folding chair, which promptly slammed shut onto floor with an echo. Jamie sighed.

"Tucker, we're going to have to ask you to leave," Ray said. Tucker responded with a distant, blank look. "Tucker? This is not the place for this behavior. Do you need someone to escort you out?"

"Betrayed," Tucker whimpered. "My best friend betrayed me." Tucker slowly pointed a finger at Jamie. "I don't need you—any of you. I'm the best member here. You're all a bunch of—"

"I don't know what you're talking about, but you need to leave," Jamie cut him off, folding his arms.

Tucker pressed his shoulder against a wall to steady himself. "This isn't over, Jamie. This isn't—" He stumbled toward the front double doors. "I'll be seeing you for my money at the end of the year. *Psh*, ten million. Newbie should just pay me my thousand bucks now." Tucker slammed the door shut behind him.

The room was silent as networkers stared at the door Tucker had just left through.

Then all at once, there was a roar of gossip.

"What was that all about?" Catherine said from behind Jamie.

"Oh God. I'm so sorry you had to see that. Listen, I don't know what—Tucker is a work-hard, play-hard type. He's probably been out all night."

Catherine raised her eyebrows. "Seems a bit over the top, don't you think? It sounded like he was threatening you."

"Yeah. Like I told you before, Tucker and I go back away. We've always had a bit of a. . . competitive dynamic in our relationship. A few weeks ago, we made a bet about how much we would sell this year. I probably got ahead of myself. It seemed like a good idea at the time."

Catherine looked thoughtful. "So you're motivating yourself by betting with Tucker?"

Jamie shrugged. "Yeah, I guess it was pretty stupid. It is a thing though."

"Tucker doesn't seem like a positive inspiration. I would think ten million dollars in sold houses would be no easy task. Especially in your first year."

"Yeah. Like I said, it was a bad idea."

"All right everyone, please. Please take a seat. Let's be professional. We'll get started in five," Ray said loudly over the chatter of networkers.

Catherine looked over to Ray at the head of the room, then back at Jamie. "Good job neutralizing the situation though. This is the type of situation we detour personally and avoid professionally." She held up a single pointer finger and lowered her voice. "You should take some time to think about that First Key, 'It's not who you know; it is always how you know them.' The right information and experience with your constituents should drive growth, not stifle professional evolution."

"The First Key," Jamie repeated.

"Given the circumstances, think about your next steps professionally. We can appreciate lofty goals, but setting a finish line is one thing. Determining how to progress is another. Reinforcement should never be negative," Catherine said with a sly, indistinct smile.

Ray approached Jamie and Catherine's corner of the conference room. "Is everything all right? Jamie, I know Tucker is your friend—"

"Yes, it's fine," Catherine interrupted. "I was just complimenting Jamie on how he handled the situation."

"Yes, thank you so much, Jamie." Ray nodded. "We'll get started."

Catherine turned back to Jamie. "I think you should have some contrast to that little outburst. Meet me at the regional airport immediately after the meeting. No need to follow me—you'll know what to do once you arrive."

"Meet you where?" Jamie looked up as Ray called again for everyone to take a seat, then down at his watch.

Catherine slid into a chair and whispered, "It's time you see how a team of professionals behaves. I'll text you the address shortly."

Ray went through the standard protocol for the meeting, and Jamie quietly took a seat opposite Catherine. He caught a glimpse out the window of Tucker slamming the door shut on a taxi.

Then he felt his phone buzz in his pocket. A text from Catherine.

"T.T: Regional Airport 38255 Mandel Dr."

He looked up at Catherine as she tucked her phone into her purse and stood for her networking commercial.

When it was LaVell's turn, he stood and walked over to where Jamie was seated. "I'm LaVell Hawkins, owner of

Dreamlightning. We're a video, photography, and digital marketing graphic art company. We at Dreamlightning help 'amplify brands to scale growth.'" He used air quotations.

"I brought in a few visual aids to show you not only my capabilities, but also what my man Jamie here produced for my wife and me." He gave Jamie a solid pat on the shoulder.

"These are some photographs I took of our old house and our new home. I wanted to contrast our living situations and highlight how simple filters can change the feeling of a scene. Before Jamie found this home for us, my wife and I lived in this house on the east side. This photo really illustrates the feeling we had living here—the spotty lawn, the chain-link fence. In contrast, if you look at this picture with a vibrant filter, you can see the trees blowing in the breeze, the three-car garage, and the welcoming entryway. This is kind of a thank-you to Jamie, an opportunity to showcase my skills, and an example of the power of design framing.

"This type of visual media has a huge impact on client perception. The more information you can get in front of customers, the more your brand sticks in their minds. Dreamlightning. Amplify your brand to scale growth."

After the meeting, Jamie made his way to LaVell. "Well done, man!"

"Thank you, thank you." LaVell chuckled and took a small bow.

"The pictures were a really nice touch. Pretty cool."

LaVell winked. "I needed to brag about how happy Cornell is now. Seriously, thanks for getting us out of our old spot. That whole car thing doesn't even compare to buying this home. Cornell and I are both really grateful for all you've done to get us through to move in. A few little tweaks, and this might be our forever home. And you know, we should team up on a few of your houses. I'll photograph them and see if I can help you get higher traffic and better offers. I got this awesome 3D camera."

Jamie smiled. "Yeah, I like that. Let me see what I have, and we'll work something out."

While LaVell chatted with an insurance broker, Jamie looked around the room. Catherine was gone. He pulled his phone out of his pocket and reopened her text.

An address. The regional airport.

Jamie put the address into his GPS as he slipped quietly out the front door.

Chapter 9

Jamie parked his car and walked into the single-terminal regional airport. No Catherine, just a few businessmen standing alongside wheeled luggage at the departures desk.

"Great," Jamie muttered.

"Hey, excuse me." He waved down a passing airport employee. "Where are the meeting rooms? I mean, your conference facilities where people meet? Sorry, I haven't been here before."

"Right down that hall and to the left." She pointed to a plain gray hallway next to baggage claim.

"Cool, thanks."

Jamie held his bag closed and jogged toward the hallway while drafting a text to Catherine.

"Here. Where are you?"

He hit "Send."

He rounded the hallway. Ceiling-to-floor windows revealed a conference-room suite.

Empty.

"So much for that."

Someone appeared at the end of the hallway.

"Excuse me, do you work here?" Jamie noted his safety jacket and neck lanyard.

"Jamie?"

"Yes. Do you. . . How do you know my name?"

"Follow me. The team left word you'd be joining."

"Oh. Right. I just figured the meeting would be here in the conference rooms."

"Most new people think that." He laughed. "No, they prefer an open-air environment."

As they rounded the corner, the runway appeared—and a long, white table with a dozen business people seated around it. The only person standing was Catherine. William Joseph Gerhard sat to her immediate left.

"Seriously. A meeting. . . on a tarmac? That's. . ."

"Absolutely. Right this way." The airport employee approached a terminal exit leading out to the tarmac. "Good luck."

The airport employee opened the door, and Jamie headed outside.

Catherine looked up as the door slammed behind him. She paused her conversation and waved at Jamie.

Jamie swallowed, and jogged the remaining yards to the table, catching his breath.

"Welcome. We're about to start this month's scrum."

"Scrum? Like in rugby?"

William Joseph laughed. "I like that. But no. Not rugby."

"Okay, well, where do I sit?"

"You can stand right there. Trusted Team standards. Privilege places people at the table," Catherine said, slipping into the last open chair.

"Privilege, huh?" Jamie looked at the people seated at the table. "So you guys are this 'Trusted Team' I keep hearing about. I thought there'd be more of you."

"More of us," William Joseph said. "Speaking of which, we'll have you sign this right now." He slid a tablet computer across the table. "Our boilerplate NDA. NDA stands for 'Nondisclosure Agreement.'"

"Got it. I know what an NDA is." Jamie drew his signature on the tablet without reading the screen. "Okay, done. Let's scrum it up." He clapped and rubbed his hands together.

"About that," Catherine started, "you'll be permitted to stay for the first part of our two-hour session this morning.

In fact, that's why I've invited you. We review applications during the second half of our meeting."

"Applications like mine?"

"You got it." William Joseph chuckled and folded his hands over his belly.

"Do we do introductions first, or—"

"No." Catherine shook her head. "We do not." She gave a short smile and cleared her throat. "Let's begin with common markets. This week I'm bringing Kaivac, my newest manufacturing client. We've integrated his software solution, so he's ready for the first campaign. Jill,"—she nodded to the straight-haired twenty-something directly across from her—"you'll set up the social and all of the ad copy. The standard known, liked, and trusted method. Jerry,"—she motioned to the man in the three-piece suit seated next to William Joseph—"can you set up the marketing automation platform, email drips, and architect the funnels? They're going to want autogenerated thank-you emails and ringless voice mail. Just logically work it into the journey. Keep a tight collaboration with Jill on this one, please. This is a new client storyboard, but a familiar vertical. He needs three landing-page designs with graphics, so we'll need a keen eye. I anticipate a rebranding upsell on this one, if we get a solid person for media."

Catherine paused and wrote on the table with a red dry-erase marker, writing her name, Jill's, and Jerry's, with lines separating the names, followed by a thick question mark.

"Thanks, Catherine." William Joseph leaned forward in his chair. "This week I'm bringing the property restoration project you all know about. Electric and HVAC contracts to Rhonda,"—he wrote her name on the table with a blue marker—"roofing, siding, and landscaping to Tyson."

The remaining Trusted Team members followed Catherine and William Joseph, calling out their newest clients and naming group members to include in the transaction. An hour later, the white table was covered in a multicolored web, each person's name with lines drawn to and from everyone else.

Jamie raised his hand. A few seconds passed before anyone noticed.

"Yes?" William Joseph raised his bushy eyebrow.

"What exactly is happening here? In this 'scrum'? You're . . . passing referrals?"

Everyone laughed.

"Yes!" William Joseph said once it calmed down. "And this,"—he held up his tablet computer—"is an abacus, not a powerful device with instant access to the world's wisdom through millions of applications."

"Still with the sarcasm. Funny guy."

"Our Third Key, I touched on previously with you," Catherine said, "'Information drives exponential growth.' We intimately understand one another's businesses. The more we know about one another's services and capabilities, the easier it is to bring one another into relationships we already have with our clients. Common markets are businesses that target the same type of account from differing business perspectives, so we start there. We move as a group. We rely on one another and support one another. And the more data we capture relating to what we've each offered to our own clients in the past, the better we connect one another with clients who we know have those exact same wants and needs. That's how our information drives exponential growth. What you see here is a week-three meeting strategically approaching a project forecasting pipeline. We rotate a four-week cycle, theming weeks in the month to define our activities."

"Giving a 'referral' is like crafting a wagon wheel," William Joseph said. "What we're doing here is more akin to designing a solar-powered rocket."

"You can see why we're so exclusive," Jill chimed in. "The Trusted Team's value is in exclusivity and scarcity. Other groups bring in professionals who want to meet customers and sell to clients. Guilds have always been about rapid revenue growth for the professional elite. We create revenue for our team, not suggest possibilities."

"To put the scrum into perspective, hundreds of thousands of dollars to millions of dollars in contracts appear on this table every month," Catherine said. "The more we know about what pie we each prefer, the bigger the slices we cut for one another. As we close out pipeline week this month, we're going to have to ask you to return to the terminal. You and I will meet again soon."

"The second hour is upon us," William Joseph said with a princess wave. "Farewell, Mr. Morris."

"Okay, well,"—Jamie pulled his messenger bag closed—"I guess I'll . . . see you next week?"

Catherine nodded. "Yes, you will."

"I'm rooting for you." William Joseph winked. "The flash cards you requested I help you with, good sir." He reached under the table for his leather briefcase. "The Illumination." William Joseph handed Jamie a little black booklet like a waiter provisioning a bottle of wine, beaming on his remark.

"The what?"

"The Illumination," every Trusted Team member echoed at once.

"You're now known, Jamie," William Joseph said. "Read the book. Put into practice the wisdom between these pages, and you'll become trusted as well as respected." William Joseph nodded, emphasizing his words. "Consider them fanciful flash cards, if you're so inclined." He was smiling.

"Um, thanks?" Jamie picked up the book with disbelief. The gold letters of the title sparkled in the sunlight. "Looks pretty classy." He flipped through the first few pages of the twenty-or-so-page book. "Quality evening reading." He slipped the book into his messenger bag. "All right then. I guess this is goodbye for now."

"Godspeed and good fortune." William Joseph nodded.

The Trusted Team members watched as Jamie backed away from the table. The meeting picked up again after a few steps.

Jamie checked his phone. Eight missed calls. Three text messages. All from Tucker.

Jamie stepped inside the terminal and read the texts.

9:11 a.m.

"How could you, man? After everything I've done for you?"

9:24 a.m.

"Come on, bro. We need each other. Let's figure this out."

9:27 a.m.

"I'm sorry, dude. I totally freaked out. Crazy night. Stripper's fault. Still friends? Answer your phone."

Jamie sighed and started typing.

"Tucker, I don't know where this is coming from. You are all over the place. I've done nothing but—"

Jamie stopped typing. He erased the message and opened his phone's contacts.

He typed Tucker's name and swallowed hard. He glanced back toward the tarmac, gritted his teeth, and pressed "Block Contact."

Chapter 10

Jamie's phone buzzed. He glanced at it while he waited for the stop light to turn green.

"Catherine. What've you got for me?" he muttered. He opened Catherine's text. "The hell?"

It was a clickable hyperlink with the text, "Trusted Team Mobile Extension."

Jamie turned into the parking lot and took the first open space. He tapped the link in the text, opening up a white web page with a single-line login.

"Huh."

He typed "/One."

"Invalid login" appeared in red letters at the top of the page.

"Guess not."

Jamie pocketed his phone and jogged up to the restaurant, the same club as their previous meeting.

"Catherine, hey!" Jamie approached her at the bar. "I was finishing up an open house. Sorry I'm a little late. Anyway, I was about to pull in and got your text." He held up his phone.

"Congratulations." She smiled after a sip of tea. "You get to play with the big boys and girls today."

"All right, that sounds vague and . . . interesting."

"Meaning it's time you contributed to your exponential growth. Jamie,"—she leaned toward him—"we're letting you test drive our framework today."

"Oh, okay. The referrals and stuff?"

"He can be taught!" Catherine smiled and turned on her own phone screen. "All you have to do is download Trusted Team's mobile extension, autofill your profile, and import contacts from every social media account you have."

"That's all, huh? Great. Easy." Jamie opened up Catherine's text again. "So, what am I missing here? How do I log in?"

"Forward slash thirteen," she said. "That's your demo credential for now. If you're accepted into the Trusted Team, you'll be our thirteenth member."

"Exciting stuff." Jamie followed her instructions, entering "Morris" on a plain black-and-white screen. Five contacts with the last name Morris popped up. Jamie scrolled through to find his name indicated by all the information he initially entered on the prospect sign-ups and all the email communications associated with his interactions with Catherine. "Wow. Is this every email and call we had?"

"Not every email, but most. The idea of a system like this is to consolidate activities with our stakeholders: suspects, prospects, customers, clients, vendors, partners. Once you get through the orientation period, you will see the tools we use to consolidate the information. The idea is to capture activities as they lead to progress. When we access the system on a laptop, I will give you a tour of the brains of our operation. We've consolidated and integrated many contributing systems to make our work go deeper and wider for our team."

"It's asking if I want to upload my contact list. Why do I need to upload my personal contacts?"

"The option is to manually add contacts or allow the system to pull in all your contacts. In the beginning, I only added contacts I chose. Every shared contact is intended to be a partner, vendor, or suspect. Suspects evolve into prospects, turning into clients as opportunities close. This means we're ready to take advantage of valuable products or services provided by our members. As we multiply our efforts to define opportunities, these prospects are escorted through the sales processes."

"Um . . . what?" Jamie chuckled. "Sorry, run that last part by me again."

"A customer for you is a potential client for everyone on the Trusted Team. A prospect for you could be a prospect for everyone else as well. Make sense?"

"Yeah, I think." Jamie accepted each profile-access permission request pop-up on his phone. "So I'm basically dumping my contacts into your guys' CRM so everyone can spam them."

Catherine set her tea down loudly. "Absolutely not. Our shared contacts database is much more than a customer-relationship-management software. If you haven't already, you'll be prompted to tag each included contact you contribute as a partner, vendor, suspect, prospect, or customer. If someone is already a customer, presumably you know what additional needs they have, as well as complimentary products or services of value, represented by our team. Our members who can provide that product or service are notified that you have a potential client for them. It's coworking evolved. The more information we input about our contacts, the faster everyone scales."

"Okay, okay," Jamie said. "You're making sense now. But hang on." He looked down at his screen. "I don't have a whole book of business yet, so what am I supposed to do about tagging my contacts? It's showing me the names of everyone I know and asking me who's a suspect, prospect, or customer."

"I'm your client. So is LaVell. He closed on his house already, correct?"

"Yeah. So, that makes him my first paying customer, technically."

"So label him as such. Later I'll show you how to open opportunities and introduce you to your sales processes. We will need to discuss how we partition and limit access. Generally we start conservative. Over the next weeks and months you'll have meetings to leverage talent of those on the team to extend and expand your marketing footprint. During this discovery process we will pin down your avatars, create a road map to disrupt attention in your specific market, implement Rethink Revenue processes, and define your first-year goals. The whole process is results-driven, focusing on activities leading to your individual definition of progress."

Jamie looked down, scrolled through his imported contacts, selected LaVell's name, and chose the customer tag. "Now it's saying to fill out his additional needs. Like what?"

"What else does he as a new home buyer need? Surely he and his wife will have ideas about renovations or additions to the property."

"Yeah, probably."

"So type that in the text field."

"Okay." Jamie typed Home Renovations. Another pop-up appeared. He turned his phone toward Catherine. "So I'm supposed to notify other members who can fulfill these needs?"

"Who do you know that renovates homes?"

"Oh, right! Mr. William Joseph Gerhard." Jamie started typing his first name, but the text field autocompleted it. "Now, that's cool! I like this a lot better than filling out slips of paper at the NAB."

"Jamie,"—Catherine smiled—"you're about to give the first real referral of your career. Moreover, a lead. But remember the Second Key, 'Setup is always better than follow-up.'"

"I saw that in *The Illumination*. Hang on. Let me write that down." Jamie pulled a pad and pencil from his messenger bag. "'Setup is always better than follow-up.' Setup has to do with referrals—er, leads? Like, setting up William Joseph and LaVell?"

"We do exchange leads. Not referrals. So, yes, you're on the right track. It's your job as the connecting party to set up both the business and the client for a successful interaction. If you do it well upfront, no follow-up should be needed. It's the difference between targeting leads for a team and loosely associating referrals with a group. If you give someone a lead, you should never have to follow up. *Ever*. Set up both people well enough so that the customer understands their skill set, and the referred professional understands the value of the project. In other words, you're connecting a buyer with a seller."

"Okay. I think I got it. How do I do that?"

"You don't." Catherine smiled. "The system does. See?" She pointed to his phone.

"Right." Jamie picked up his phone again. The confirmation page on his screen featured an email template with both LaVell and William Joseph as recipients. The message subject line read, "LaVell, meet William Joseph. William Joseph, meet LaVell." The message itself read, "Hello, LaVell and William Joseph. I don't think you know each other yet, but you should. LaVell, since you recently purchased a new home and are looking to make renovations, I would like to formally introduce you to William Joseph. William Joseph is a general contractor. You'll both get a lot of value from a conversation, so I'm reaching out to both of you to facilitate a meeting."

"Wow!" Jamie said. "It's a one-click referral. I mean lead." He clicked the "Send" button. The screen flashed a sent notification.

"As the Second Key reads, 'Setup is always better than follow-up.'" Catherine smiled. "I'll leave you to it. You have a lot of tagging to do. When you've finished, the system will notify me, and you'll be ready for the next step."

"Let me guess." Jamie smirked. "I'll find out what that is when I'm 'ready'?" He made sarcastic air quotes. "I'm starting to get used to the cryptic instructions, Catherine. You can't surprise me anymore."

"You're confident. That's not a bad thing, but don't let your confidence blind you from what you don't know. So then, you've read *The Illumination* to completion?"

"The what? Oh, right!" Jamie's hand slid over his messenger bag. "Of course. I read it. I mean, a lot of it. I kind of, you know, skimmed."

Catherine shook her head slowly. "If you want to know where this is going, read it. No skimming." She took one more sip of tea. "Until next time, Mr. Jamie." Smiling, she turned and walked out of the restaurant.

"Bye, Catherine," Jamie called after her.

A waiter approached the table. "What can I get for you, sir?"

"I'll have some coffee. No, sorry, tea. I'll um, have a cup of tea, please. I've got some reading to do." He pulled out *The Illumination* and set it face-down on his bag.

"Cream or sugar?"

Jamie glanced down at Catherine's cup and saw no empty packets. "No, just black, er regular. You know what I mean."

"Indeed. Very good, sir."

Jamie scrolled through his contacts. The next name that popped up made him jump. Tucker. "Great. I guess the Trusted Team doesn't care about blocked contacts." He hovered over the three different tag options—no, four options. He tapped Skip Contact.

"All right, Cath, what do you have for me?" Jamie set his phone to silent and picked up the book. He whispered the single sentence on the first page. "'Ignite Net Worth by Evolving Networking.' Huh. Good stuff."

He turned the page.

"Illuminating the Trusted Team: Creating more by positioning yourself in the right environment to foster growth is key to lifelong success. The relationships you build should positively affect your strength, evolve your perspective, and nourish your spirit. By complementing your efforts with like-minded individuals, you set a new standard for your trajectory. Own your future by realizing potential and that of your Trusted Team."

Jamie flipped to page three.

The Five Keys of the Trusted Team.

1. *It's Not Who You Know; It's How You Know Them*

2. *Setup Is Always Better Than Follow-Up*

3. *Information Drives Exponential Growth*

4. *The Second Sale Is Always Easier than the First*

5. *Accountability Goes Both Ways*

He looked over both of his shoulders.

"It's about damn time. Flash cards."

Chapter 11

"The Fifth Key," Jamie read aloud. "Accountability goes both ways."

He pulled a yellow highlighter out of his messenger bag and marked the Fifth Key in the table of contents.

"Page five."

Jamie flipped through the pages and read the key's subtitle under his breath. "Communicate with strategic partners, and those we serve, to drive business."

He chuckled. "How . . . illuminating."

"Any Trusted Team member who shares a lead is accountable for completing the introduction between both parties. What differentiates leads from referrals is qualification and follow-through. A team member closes a qualified lead relatively on the spot, whereas referrals still need 'qualification workflow.' Members save valuable time by connecting sellers with buyers who are ready to close and vice-versa."

Jamie put down the book and checked the Trusted Team system on his phone.

"So I guess one email isn't good enough," he whispered. He opened the calendar app on his phone.

Drop off thank-you gift at LaVell's, 2:00 p.m.

The clock on his phone read 12:57.

"Close enough."

Jamie packed up, paid his bill, and left the restaurant. He opened the ice chest in his trunk and pulled out a golden box of chocolates. He loosened the red ribbon around it and peeked inside.

"No melting. Still good."

Jamie punched his first sale's address into his GPS and drove the twenty minutes in silence.

Ding-dong. Jamie pressed the couple's new doorbell once.

"Jamie!" LaVell swung open the door. "You're early."

"Never look a gift horse in the mouth." Jamie jiggled the box under his arm. "Can I come in?"

"Sure, yeah, c'mon in. Cornell's just in the kitchen finishing up dishes."

"Thanks."

"Oh, wait." LaVell stopped Jamie before his first step inside. "New house, man. You're wearing your good socks, right?"

"So, no shoes."

"Yes sir." LaVell smiled. "Just put 'em by the door here." He pointed to a shoe rack next to the door.

"Of course." Jamie handed LaVell the box of chocolates and untied his laces. "I can't really stay long. I just wanted to drop this off with you two."

"Why, thank you for the candy. Cornell and I are doing this low-carb, slow-carb diet thing. That chocolate will come in handy on cheat day." LaVell peeked around the corner into the kitchen, then leaned in to Jamie. "Which is every day for me."

"Gotcha." Jamie winked.

"Cornell, look who's early!" LaVell announced. "Jamie brought us some sweets."

"Jamie, hey!" Cornell peered around the corner while sudsing up a plate. "Why didn't you tell me we had company?"

"'Cause he just got here?"

"Actually, I really can't stay long," Jamie said. "I just wanted to thank both of you. You know, in person. It was a real pleasure helping you guys get this place. It already looks so homey. So the move-in went well?"

"Yeah, Cornell's parents came up and helped with packing. Wasn't too hard since we really only had bedroom stuff and furniture for the main level here. You saw how small that old place was," LaVell said.

"Hey!" Jamie snapped his fingers. "That reminds me. I sent you an email about some of the improvements around the house you've talked about doing. Did you get that?"

LaVell pulled out his smartphone. "Doesn't sound familiar. When did you send it?"

"Earlier today. So I was thinking about setting you up with a guy who can pretty much do anything you guys need. Like bathroom updates, wall treatments, mantelpiece refinishing, whatever. Is that still something you want to do?"

"One hundred percent granite countertops in the bathrooms to match the kitchen. And I really want to get some reclaimed wood on the fireplaces. Possibly some built-in shelving in the entryway for shoes," Cornell said. "We've been saving up to get everything just right. Who's your guy?"

"His name is William Joseph Gerhard," Jamie said. "I'm already working with him on a rehab project. He's got attention to detail you probably won't see anywhere else. I'd trust the guy with my family's place."

"Great! Oh, here's your email." LaVell scrolled through his inbox. "Yep. 'Meet William Joseph.' Cool."

"Awesome. You'll love him. You'll love his work. He's a master carpenter. You'll see what I mean." Jamie nodded.

"Sorry to cut things short, but I've got another appointment to run to."

"Oh, no worries." LaVell put his phone away. "We'll definitely set something up with William." He walked Jamie to the door. "Thanks for stopping by!"

"You got it, LaVell." Jamie slipped his shoes back on. "And let me know how it goes with William Joseph. Oh! That's another thing. He goes by William Joseph, not William or Will. Trust me, that is good information to have. I'll see you at the NAB."

"Cool. Yeah, I'll let you know."

"Catch you later." Jamie stepped out onto the porch.

"Hey, Jamie? Hold up."

"What?"

"Have you talked to Tucker recently?"

"Why would you ask *me* that?" Jamie fake-chuckled.

"So you haven't." LaVell leaned against the doorframe and crossed his arms. "Listen. He reached out to have coffee."

"Par. What did he think of you turning him down? After what happened at—"

"We already met."

"Hmm. Oh. Well. How'd that go?"

"He wanted to talk about the car I'm not going to buy." LaVell's tone lightened. "You know how he is. 'There's this car at the dealership I have to put you in.'"

"Again par for the course. Classic Tucker."

"We also talked about you."

"Me? Why? How'd I come up?"

"He's really wanting to patch things up."

"What did he say?"

"Look, I don't want to get between—"

"What exactly did he say?"

"I just think you guys should reconnect. It'll be good for you. And him."

"Tucker's not going to make it. I get it, okay?" Jamie stared past LaVell. "We've all been on the same ship for a long time now, but he's continually going too far."

"You're right about that. Come on, we all know Tucker's just being a dick. He admits it. That's his thing. The guy's done a lot for us over the years, and now the NAB and whatnot. We're all coming up together."

"Yeah, and I think I've outgrown Tucker. Period."

"Just talk to the guy."

"No, I'm good. Time to level up." Jamie turned away. "I've come into my own. All that drama takes my time and dilutes my focus. You had a roommate before Cornell, right?"

"Cornell's not my roommate. We're married."

"Ha. Funny. Right. You know what I mean." Jamie had a deadpan look.

"Seriously, though. Yeah, I did have a roommate."

"Remember what that was like. Now replace that roommate with Tucker. It's like he and I've been roommates all of our adult lives. You know what? I'm done. It's time to move out and get my own place. You and your old roommate—did you have that unspoken rule that you don't go into each other's bedrooms without knocking or asking first?"

"Of course."

"Well, I've closed my door, but Tucker keeps barging in. I'm doing my own thing now. I've moved out."

"All right then."

Jamie shifted foot to foot while he and LaVell looked past each other.

"But hey, I appreciate you looking out."

"Any time."

The two pound-hugged.

"Hey, don't forget." Jamie pointed at LaVell. "He goes by William Joseph."

"You got it."

"Bye now." Jamie stepped off the porch and waved back.

The second LaVell shut the front door, Jamie dialed William Joseph. He picked up halfway into the first ring.

"William Joseph speaking. Hello, Jamie."

"Hey! Did you happen to get my email from earlier?"

"Yes, I did. Are they—" A loud buzz cut him off. "Sorry, got you on the headset. I'm installing Catherine's new chandelier. By new, I mean it's less than one hundred years old. You don't want to know the price a vintage chandelier fetches at auction."

"Hell no. So anyway, I was just—"

Another buzz.

"Hello? Hello?"

"Sorry. I'm on a timetable," William Joseph said. "What are you calling about again?"

"LaVell and Cornell. I referred them to you in the email."

"Ah, yes. Bully for you. Was that your first lead submitted through our system?"

"Yeah, it was. And I'm calling to let you know that yes, they are in fact ready to buy, it sounds like. Cornell said they've been saving up. She wants some work in her bathrooms done to match her kitchen granite countertops. Add some reclaimed wood to the fireplace. And she needs a solution in the foyer for shoes. Sounds like a perfect project for a master carpenter!"

"Holding yourself accountable. I respect it." A third buzz. "So they want natural-stone solid surface counters. Not quartz, but granite?"

"Yeah, that's what is in the kitchen. You'll see the type of granite when you come over. Just meet up with them and close the sale. You're all set up."

"Excellent. I'll thank you if we come to an agreement. Fine work, young sir."

"Well, like I said, they're already sold, basically."

"I appreciate a lead, but—damn it! Odin's beard, that smarts!"

Jamie laughed under his breath. "You okay?"

Crackling came from William Joseph's phone.

"William Joseph? Are you okay?"

"*Ugh*. Yes." A fifth and longer buzz. "Have you ever installed a manual lever to hoist seventy kilograms?"

"No. I don't even know what that means."

"Good. Don't try it."

"All right, I'll leave it to the experts. Sounds above my skill set."

"One could not even imagine."

"Nope, I guess not. Can you check in with me once you get something on the schedule to talk to LaVell and Cornell?"

"Yes, I commit to following up with you by phone or by air."

"By air?" Jamie laughed. "Sure. Either way. I'll talk to you later."

William Joseph's follow-up came the next morning.

Sunday morning.

At seven a.m.

Jamie's phone vibrated itself off the nightstand. He answered without looking at the caller's name.

"This is Jamie." His voice cracked, and he cleared his throat. "Hello?"

"William Joseph speaking. Are you occupied?"

"No, I was just, um . . ." Jamie sat up in bed, turned his lamp on, and yawned.

"Sleeping? A full hour after sunrise?"

"What? It's Sunday."

"That's neither here nor there. I spoke with LaVell and Cornell last night. We had dinner together."

"Oh, wow. That was fast. Dinner with them?"

"Yes. You were right. I didn't have to sell them anything. We bantered, ate casserole, and I gave a quote on the spot. They didn't balk at the price, Cornell signed, and I left before nine. She's a snazzy one. She knows exactly what she wants."

"That's great! So I had the sale in the bag for you. Qualified lead, no softening up needed."

"Correct. Thank you. A fine job."

"You bet."

"One other thing, Jamie. Chocolates. Really?"

"What?"

"I applaud the effort, but please. Not very original. You're telling the client you care, but not very much."

"Seriously? They're just chocolates. They really meant a lot to LaVell."

"Then why did they send the unopened box home with me? The opera creams were delicious, by the way."

"Hey, they're on a diet. I didn't know. It's the thought that counts."

"Touché."

"I'll do fruit or something next time."

"Slightly better. Unrelated topic. Have you spoken with Catherine lately?"

"Define 'lately.'"

"In the last twelve hours."

"Dude, it's the weekend. I'm usually busy showing houses. I've got like three or four today alone."

"That's a no then."

"Yeah, no. We haven't talked. Like I said, I'm busy on the weekends."

"You can't be that busy if you're not awake by sunrise."

"There's still enough time in the day for what I have to do."

"Suit yourself. Again, thank you for the lead. I'll leave you to your morning nap. Expect a call from Catherine by tonight."

"Okay. Whatever. Sure."

"Farewell." William Joseph hung up.

Jamie tossed his phone on the end of the bed and collapsed backward between two pillows.

Another phone call vibrated his phone.

"Not again."

Jamie sat up and reached for his phone. LaVell's name appeared.

"Hey, man!" Jamie answered. "How's it going?"

"Oh, we're great. You said you wanted me to call after we talked to William Joseph. I hope I'm not calling too early."

"Oh, no. I'm just—" Jamie pulled the phone back and checked the time. 7:28 a.m. "I'm just making coffee." He rolled off the bed and stumbled to his studio's kitchenette. "How'd it go? Tell me what happened."

"Yeah, so he really is a great guy. Cornell asked him to stay for dinner, and he showed us these before-and-after pics on his catalog website. He seems like a capable contractor. He—yeah, honey? Yeah, I'll tell him. I'll—Jamie?"

"Yeah? Was that Cornell?"

"She says to tell you she likes him, besides him being a weird little gnome man."

"All that's missing is a red hat!" Cornell shouted in the background.

"Ha! Should I pass on the fashion idea?"

"No, no!" LaVell laughed. "We're good. He was a little short and hairy is all."

"That and he talks funny . . . but good people."

"You can say that again." LaVell laughed once more.

"Aside from that, it sounds like he's the right contractor for you. I'm super glad."

"Definitely. We appreciate it. Thanks again, Jamie. Take care."

"One lead down. Time to find another one," Jamie muttered. As he made coffee, he opened the Trusted Team app and started scrolling through his contacts.

Knock. Knock. Knock.

Jamie checked the time. 7:49 a.m.

"Who would come to my door before eight in the morning on a freakin' Sunday?" Jamie asked aloud. He glanced down at the T-shirt and shorts he'd slept in. "Good enough."

He opened the door.

"Good morning, Jamie."

Catherine.

"Hi. Hey. I mean, good morning! Sorry, it's just . . . a little early. Come in. What are you doing here?"

Catherine didn't move from the doorway. "I don't have much time to explain, there's—did you sleep in that? Never mind. I'll give you ten minutes. Please meet me at my car. I'll be parked one block over." She gestured toward the street and walked away.

Jamie was silent as he shut the door. "What the hell? Why does everything have to be so weird? And . . . why am I always surprised?" He hurried to the bathroom.

Three knocks came in succession.

"She forget something?" Jamie rolled his eyes.

"Jamie?" called a muffled voice. "Dude, are you home?"

Tucker.

Chapter 12

Tucker exhaled and flicked his cigarette hard, sending it tumbling down the sidewalk.

"So,"—Jamie swallowed—"what's up?"

"How're sales?"

"Seriously? That's weak." Jamie stepped back, leaving the front door open. "You show up here randomly on a Sunday morning to ask me how sales are?"

"Seriously. You must be up to something." Tucker sipped his steaming gas-station coffee. "I saw Catherine rolling out. She stay overnight?"

"What?" Jamie glanced in the direction Catherine had left. No sign of her. "She just randomly showed up here this morning. Same as you and all the other people who want to bother me at the crack of dawn on a Sunday."

"Riiiiight. You two are, you know,"—Tucker made an obscene gesture—"just like that, huh?"

"You hit your head? What the hell is wrong with you?" Jamie stepped back and pushed the door shut.

"Wait!" Tucker put his hand on the door.

"What? What do you *really* want?"

"Can I come in? I want to—"

"No, I don't think that's a good idea, actually."

"'Look, I'm not mad about you hooking up with Catherine."

"That's it. Conversation over." Jamie slammed the door again.

"C'mon, man!" Tucker shouted. "Please! Let me talk to you."

Jamie opened the door two inches. "This is your last chance, Tucker. Be serious."

Tucker sipped his coffee and held up his index finger. "One question. Okay? Same as before. How're sales?"

"What do you mean?"

"I mean the bet, Jamie. You forget?"

"Oh. No, of course not. I just don't think it's worth seeing you for the rest of the year to get my money."

"So? How close are you to ten mill? You cut me out of your life like some ex you don't care about. The least you can do is tell me your score. It's the right thing to do after everything you did."

"*I did?* Really? It's my fault you constantly embarrass me? It's my fault you act like networking is happy hour on singles night? Seriously?"

"Dude, keep it down. You're making an ass of yourself in front of the world."

"*Nobody's here!* The neighbors are normal people who are still sleeping! You know what? This is stupid. I don't have to take this. If you're just here 'cause you're worried about paying me at the end of the year, you're off the hook."

"Hook? What h—"

Jamie slammed the door again. "Where's my freakin' bag? Oh." He grabbed his messenger bag off the lone coat hook by the door and rummaged through it for his checkbook. "Here." Jamie swung the door wide open, startling Tucker. "I'm giving you one thousand bucks right now." He furiously filled out the first check. "You win. Okay? Bet's over." Jamie tore the check out, wadded it up, and threw it at Tucker. "If this is the reason you're here, take the money and leave. A little pocket money for your next trip to Aruba, Jamaica, or wherever else you're flying to next. Cocktails on me! Now get out of here and move on." Jamie slammed the door one last time, locked the deadbolt, slid on a pair of noise-cancelling headphones, and got dressed.

After one full minute, he peered through the peephole. No Tucker. Just a crushed Styrofoam coffee cup on the lawn.

Jamie checked the clock on the wall. "I gotta move."

Jamie wet his hand, once-covered his hair, and grabbed his bag on his way out the door. A short jog later, he arrived at Catherine's idling Infiniti SUV.

"Cath. Hey, sorry . . . I just . . . I . . . had, um . . . unexpected company." Jamie wheezed.

"Tucker?"

"Uh-huh. You saw him?"

"He slithered by me. The NAB won't miss him. Want to hop in? Let's take a drive."

"Sure. A little perspective would be nice. Where to?"

"Wherever the road takes us. I enjoy driving on the weekends. It helps me clear my head."

Jamie climbed into the passenger seat and tucked his bag between his legs.

"Put that in the back," Catherine said. "And buckle your seat belt."

"Oh. Um, sure."

Catherine pulled away from the curb. "You've now read *The Illumination* cover to cover."

"Is that a question?"

"No."

"Oh. Yes, I did read the book."

"Then you know the Trusted Team does not grant membership until such time as applicants identify and nominate another professional."

"Yeah, I think I remember something about that."

"Been skimming again, have we?"

"No, I read it! Okay, fine, I got through like, everything except the last few pages. I've been busy showing houses."

"I'll let you slide . . . again." Catherine took a sip from her mug. Tea tags dangled from the side. "Do you think you have enough of a handle on the mechanisms driving our little machine to identify a prospective member to invite?"

"I think so. That's part of being a member, recruiting prospects? Like the NAB?"

"No, not exactly. Recruit means you enlist someone. We discover or identify. We need quality, complementary team members. We believe certain professionals flourish in our environment, while others wouldn't be able to appreciate our team's focus. The final step in evolving from prospect to member is to show your ability to identify our qualities in others. Your nominee may or may not join, depending on their interests. We just need to see that you've acquired an eye for extending the vision of the Trusted Team. Make sense?"

Jamie paused, fiddling with a pen in his hand. "Is it common to invite friends, or is mixing professional and personal relationships frowned upon?"

"The nature of our group focuses on relationship development. Hence the First Key, 'It's not who you know; it's how you know them.' If you feel there's a case for an acquaintance to be introduced to the team, however, we aren't going to discriminate against good opportunity."

"I was thinking about LaVell. Remember what he said in his last NAB commercial? About making your brand stick by providing customers with more information?"

"I recall."

"He's a sharp guy with a unique skill set. I didn't really understand what he did until he offered me direction on personal branding. He's really opened my eyes to the way people perceive value. Plus, he's an all-around cool guy."

Catherine paused at a stop sign and turned on her windshield wipers as raindrops began to fall. "So, LaVell. Not Tucker?"

"Yeah, no. Unfortunately, I've realized some people encourage and inspire me to do my best work, while others just wait to kick me when I'm down. Tucker's in my rearview mirror."

Catherine sipped her tea. "We all go through transitions to become better versions of ourselves. Sometimes personal growth has casualties. Whether personally or professionally, the people we know today need to affect us in a positive manner. Trusting in oneself and one's social and professional circles adds strength while propelling us forward."

Jamie glanced down at his pen. "Yeah. Not Tucker."

They sat in silence for a moment.

"I had a discussion with William Joseph," Catherine spoke up. "Just so you know, he agrees LaVell is a possible prospect also."

"Really?"

"Yes. Absolutely. William Joseph recognizes LaVell's potential, same as you. You've chosen well. With William Joseph's recent interactions, my association, and now your recommendation, LaVell would certainly be a solid person to reveal our team to. Personally, I've always thought highly of him."

"What's next then? Are you or William Joseph going to talk to him?"

Catherine raised her eyebrow.

Jamie looked down. "I guess I missed that part, too, huh? Full disclosure, Catherine—I'm an audiobook kind of guy. Reading has never been my highest priority."

"That is becoming apparent. Open the glove box."

"Why? What's in there?"

"Your future."

Jamie opened the glove box.

"This?" He pulled out a small vintage brass box.

"Yes."

"Open it."

Jamie pulled the top off the box. Nestled inside was a stack of thick black Trusted Team business cards.

"Your future is promising, Jamie. Welcome to the team."

Jamie lifted the top card out of the tight stack. He flipped the card back and forth, and the words *Trusted.Team* glinted in the light from the cloudy sky. On the opposite side of the card, he touched the raised number in the lower right corner.

"Slash thirteen," he read.

LaVell sat alone at the table nearest the door, filling out his triplicate referral slips for the week. NAB networkers inched forward in line for breakfast.

"Morning!" Jamie gave his shoulder a friendly slap. "How's business this week?"

"Hey, Jamie. It's rolling along. You?" As the line shortened, LaVell stood up and stepped in line for coffee and donuts.

"Excellent." Jamie laid his messenger bag on the table. "Hey, LaVell? Um, actually, I think I forgot something in my car. I'll be right back."

"Cool. I'll save you a seat. You want coffee?"

"No coffee. Thanks."

After waiting in line for a few minutes, LaVell pushed down on the air pot, releasing a steaming stream of coffee into his cup.

Knock. Knock. Knock.

LaVell jerked his head toward the sound. "What the hell?"

He looked around. No one was standing where the sound had come from.

"Huh. Okay."

LaVell grabbed two donuts, balanced them on his coffee cup, and headed back to his spot at the table. As he carefully set down his breakfast, something on the table reflected light. LaVell reached across the table and picked up a thick black business card. A debossed title in wide gold lettering read, "Trusted.Team."

"Huh." LaVell flipped the card over, revealing a raised number in the lower right corner—"/Thirteen."

"Come on, Tucker," LaVell whispered. "This again?"

Jamie walked up to the table and tucked a pen in his blazer jacket.

"Hey, Jamie," LaVell said. "Have you seen Tucker sneaking around in here this morning? I think he banged on the table after leaving this card. Isn't this the same one you got a while back?" LaVell backhanded the card and took a bite of donut.

Jamie pulled the card from LaVell's fingers.

"Yeah, man, looks like it." Jamie inspected. "Yep, same type card. Mine had slash one on the back instead of slash thirteen."

"Tucker showed me the one he said you got. Something about some weird website." LaVell shrugged. "I don't really remember what it was he was saying. He seemed kinda pissed you got onto it. What ended up happening with that whole thing?"

"Tucker told you about the card and the website and everything?"

"Yeah man, you know how he is, got all, 'Jamie comes to one meeting and gets this card from someone at the NAB, and I get left out.' He showed me the card, and I told him about the dot team domain being like dot com. told him to try running an internet search on 'trusted dot team' to see if anything came up."

"Huh. Interesting. Did you go to the site?"

"No, I never thought about it after we talked. You know how he is. He's always gotta be the man." LaVell chuckled.

"Yeah, it's unfortunate. But you're exactly right. He's always been that way. He'll never change. Or evolve. Let's just move on and then up from that, LaVell." Jamie gave his shoulder a friendly slap. "But to answer your question, it's a real site, and you should go to it. The card is an invitation. Pull up the site, and you'll see what I'm talking about."

LaVell took another bite.

"Seriously, pull your phone out right now."

"Okay, okay." LaVell wiped his sugar-powdered fingers on a napkin.

"Type in," Jamie said, "*Trusted.Team.*"

Eyes wide, LaVell pulled out his smartphone.

Afterword

Trusted.Team is a true story of experiences we've all felt in some form. This story of personal growth through sacrifice isn't a new concept. Hopefully, thoughts of your unique experiences accompanied you right here, right now in this book. The truth is we all have forces, positive and negative, that are allowed to influence our journeys. The choices we make and adventures we choose make us who we are today. If you reread and imagine yourself as each character in this story (for better or worse), you'll find we've all been somebody's Tucker or somebody's Catherine. Somebody liked as Jamie or loved like Cornell. We are all eccentric. We all take pride in something like William Joseph Gerhard with his coveted skills. We are all a mix of these characters, influencing or being influenced by the roles people play.

Ultimately, I wrote this novel to illustrate an evolved approach to business, specifically the human side of organized business relationships. The specific personalities and situations throughout the book are sourced from personal life experiences. Like you, I've trudged forward through heartbreaking dissociations while at the same time being enlightened by unlikely characters. All experiences considered, from my Jamie or LaVell perspective, I would have appreciated recognition for my unique abilities. As

Catherine, I would love to build something that unifies people to achieve their goals. As Tucker, I would have loved to be understood for who I am, even at my worst times, by people who truly cared for me.

Becoming a professional is a quest. It's not something we just wake up and do. Initially, I thought this book would be a case study about how to properly use customer-relationship-management software. In the end we have an introspective case study of the human condition. Fundamentally, this story starts to unravel truth behind struggling people finding common ground to go on a very personal and professional journey together. Through the creative process to explain how system selling can affect a group of people, I discovered maxims I didn't know we could live by.

Bringing this book full circle, what if there really was an organization that supported evolving to higher standards?

What if I shared a vision with people who want to take ownership of their own success and we banded together?

Is it possible that a group of individuals is out there creating value for one another while simultaneously weaving together strengths on a team, in a system, with a playbook?

All of this starts with the keys laid out in *The Illumination*—the Trusted.Team handbook companion to this business fable—supporting that realization for everyone. It's all about complementary perspectives. The Trusted.

Team concept caters to the journey others are on to find us, rather than our agenda to gain more for ourselves. It's about the value you want to give based on the value you're seeking. Simply put, we can't offer *all* the value, but we know people who can.

The way I look at it, businesses do business with hundreds of us. Just thin offices separate us. As far as I know, I'm working with the same company you're calling on today. If you knew our shared prospect had an upcoming birthday or loved old motorcycles, how valuable would that be? If you knew me, liked me, and trusted me as a professional, we could easily work together to the same end. We could accelerate to the value-added, trusted-partner designation, working together because we could multiply our efforts. This is how the idea of coworking translates into the method, or keys, lived by the Trusted.Team.

Start at the beginning by taking a hard look at personal relationships developed over the course of our lives and compare them to professional goals. Decisions must be made.

To get the information we need, we have to understand one another. The Five Keys are tenets the Trusted.Team shares, a common standard. As the saying goes, "Don't tell me; show me." My hope is this story does just that: shows you what could be possible if a path forward reveals itself. If you can see the path, are you able to step into the light to become more than you ever thought you could?

I say take the next step and understand the business focus *The Illumination* brings to this book. After you get the keys, start your professional evolution by rereading Chapter 3. Everything you need to turn your unique potential into momentum is hiding in plain sight. Together, we make it happen.

The Illumination:

the Manifesto of the Trusted.Team

Mission

Evolve Networks to Ignite Net Worth

Philosophy

Discovering people whose knowledge amplifies their drive to be value-added is special. In a coworking effort, we actively commit to evolve personal networks of expert-level resources into well-defined, results-driven strategic partnerships. Each member contributes to the framework, lacing closely tied relationships and selectively shared information. Membership of this "mastermind" of strategic partnerships is exclusive.

With business networking origins, strategic partners drive engagement to one another by becoming conscious of our customer's journey. Our team members support one another with a standardized process designed to build momentum and expand resources. Trusted.Team is purpose-driven, built on the success of individual members. We curate people who will succeed through attainable goals and execution on collective standards.

Standard Keys

1. It's Not Who You Know; It's How You Know Them

2. Setup is Always Better than Follow-Up

3. Information Drives Exponential Growth

4. The Second Sale is Always Easier than the First

5. Accountability Goes Both Ways

It's Not Who You Know;
It's How You Know Them

Elaboration

Interpersonal relationships are complicated. Breathe life into yours with purpose and consideration. As your network is your net worth, personal associations reflect your professionalism. A keen understanding of those who surround you is of the utmost importance. As a team should be accountable and a positive influence, we highlight character. Symbiotic relationships form interlocking circles of trust, so we must always work to nurture fertile ground. Intentional growth projects a standard of always reaching for more. Ambitious endeavors should always be supported by those with creative minds, forward-looking mentalities, and the metal to hold those around them accountable.

Exemplified

Purpose is created in relationships.

Setup is Always Better than Follow-Up

Elaboration

People ask for references without knowing the value of resources. Believe in the introduction built on your merit to drive a proliferated team. Standard professionalism has a degree of follow-up associated with it yet overlooks the initial setup. First impressions capitalize on elements of surprise when identifying an opportunity. Since value propositions depend on knowledge and presentation, make an impressive introduction with knowledge of your team's level of service. Open a prospective client to the possibilities afforded them when they do business within the team's circle. Driving home the value of trust within the lead discovery releases momentum echoed through to follow-up. Because your partners agree to a plan, be the initial stage in the predetermined process.

Exemplified

First impressions create valuable momentum.

Information Drives Exponential Growth

Elaboration

Data is slippery and nebulous if it is not properly recorded. Nurture transparency with historical proof. Data is the highest valued asset anyone exchanges. By uniformly consolidating information and creating an organizational system to framework it, we create a powerful growth. Everyday people contribute contact points in communication channels. We categorize every contact point our members contribute to create more opportunities for everyone. We define customer journeys to distill our value so our potential increases with every data point we identify.

Exemplified

Data fuels progress.

The Second Sale is Always Easier than the First

Elaboration

Creating an honest relationship leads to referent power, so aim to be the subject-matter expert (SME) with a strong supporting cast. Creating an honest, transparent, and trusted relationship is done through integrity. This relationship naturally makes you the first person they think of when talking to others about your area of expertise. Becoming a subject-matter expert takes study and diligence, keeping yourself abreast of changes in your field, and knowing the risks and rewards of choices, options, and competitors. Being seen as an SME further solidifies both your standing with clients as well as your supporting cast. As each of your Trusted.Team members strengthens their position as an SME, you form a stronger and more powerful stance as a team.

Growing as a subject-matter expert is the process of moving from being a "known resource" to a "liked resource" and finally to a "trusted resource." This process takes time. When one of your fellow Trusted.Team members has achieved trusted status with a client and introduces them to you, another SME they trust, you serve the client from an elevated position. Businesses are going to consume products and services. We have a duty as value-added resources to introduce quality. Invite team members to complement your client's business. A parallel team member's first sale to your client is your second sale.

Exemplified

Known, liked, and trusted is the gold standard.

Accountability Goes Both Ways

Elaboration

Communicate with strategic partners, and those we serve, to drive business. Any Trusted Team member who shares a lead is accountable for completing the introduction between both parties. What differentiates leads from referrals is qualification and follow-through. A team member closes a qualified lead relatively on the spot, whereas referrals still need 'qualification workflow.' Members save valuable time by connecting sellers with buyers who are ready to close and vice-versa.

Exemplified

Give and expect communication because it is the standard.

Referrals are the fuel driving networking. In contrast, strategic partners drive business to one another by empowering value-added team members with consolidated information. By leveraging the game within the game, strategic partnerships are supported with a standardized targeting process designed to drive momentum.

Starting with the Five Standard Keys, our partnerships capitalize on IT innovation, evolve individual businesses, and forge group goals. How we make it happen together starts with a simple method of Discover, Disrupt, and Rethink.

Discover.

By purposefully designing professional standards, we separate ourselves from the constraints of business as usual. The voyage to higher quality starts with observing true value and seeking mutual advantage. This is fundamentally our story and the journey of those we associate with personally and professionally. Always start at the beginning.

Disrupt.

Creating a new path is all about change. Inwardly and outwardly, reality is intelligently designed to plan out attention on a new trajectory. This is where we find commonality among unique approaches. Offensively interrupt attention. Create an unseen course of action.

Rethink.

Gathering up combined experience and agreeing to leverage skills that multiply effort, we see the world with a new vision. By treating every experience leading to this moment as a test, we can drive our own success. Where we start never dictates our finish. Forging success into the everyday is about challenging the norm. Change perspective, define reality.

Creating revenue in today's business climate is much different than days gone by. Understanding a principled approach to a unified sales process takes logical, detailed thought, supported by all the resources available to us today. Agreeing to zoom out to a perspective where working on the business creates efficiencies on every level within the business is the most effective way to attain annual goals.

In the coming weeks, you will be asked to think about your business as a series of key performance indicators. Comparing historical activities leading to your definition of progress will be the focus. We want to establish some ground work to determine how you will shape the future. Our business is your business, so by creating a solid road map, we can drive toward attainable goals.

Together We Make It Happen!